This book is a

Gift

From

....

To

....

Date

....

May God bless you through this book

PRAYERS TO KEEP YOUR MARRIAGE OUT OF TROUBLE

PRAYERS TO KEEP YOUR MARRIAGE OUT OF TROUBLE

PRAYER M. MADUEKE

PRAYERS TO KEEP YOUR MARRIAGE OUT OF TROUBLE

Copyright © 2011

PRAYER M. MADUEKE

ISBN:

Prayer Publications

Unless otherwise indicated, all Scripture quotations are taken from the King James Version of the Bible, and used by permission. All emphasis within quotations is the author's additions.

First Edition, 2011

Printed in the U.S.A

For further information of permission

1 Babatunde close, off Olaitan Street, Surulere, Lagos, Nigeria
+234 803 353 0599
Email: pastor@prayermadueke.com,
Website: www.prayermadueke.com

Table of Contents

Chapter 1

HOSTILITIES IN MARRIAGE

One of the most significant challenges in the world today is marriage unrest, which often results to collapse. Many displaced marriages today are in hands of manipulators and marriage breakers. What used to be the most admirable institution on earth, ordained by God, is fast becoming a mockery. Devil and his forces have invaded millions of prosperous homes. Many ongoing conflicts and hostilities in marriages today are all evil designs.

'Therefore I say unto you, Take no thought for your life, what ye shall eat, or what ye shall drink; nor yet for your body, what ye shall put on. Is not the life more than meat, and the body than raiment? Behold the fowls of the air: for they sow not, neither do they reap, nor gather into barns; yet your heavenly Father feedeth them. Are ye not much better than they? Which of you by taking thought can add one cubit unto his stature? And why take ye thought for raiment? Consider the lilies of the field, how they grow; they toil not, neither do they spin' (Matthew 6:25-28).

The truth is that men have abandoned God. Anxiety and greed have taken over hearts of men. Majority of people on earth today have no reverence or regard for personal experiences with God. Men take thoughts for their lives and eschew dependence on God. They ignore God to pursue personal goals without considering God's Word on how He wants men to live on earth. Most people are preoccupied with what they will eat, drink and put on without knowing or caring at all why they are here on earth. They do many things to survive, without God.

'Wherefore, if God so clothe the grass of the field, which today is, and tomorrow is cast into the oven, shall he not much more clothe you, O ye of little faith? Therefore take no thought, saying, What shall we eat? Or, what shall we drink? Or, wherewithal shall we be clothed? (For after all these things do the Gentiles seek) for your heavenly Father knoweth that ye have need of all these things. But seek ye first the kingdom

of God, and his righteousness; and all these things shall be added unto you' (Matthew 6:30-33).

If you know God, keep His commandments, and He will surely give you all good things you desire. Our first duty on earth is not to fight for our needs. We need God, His Kingdom and righteousness first, and every other thing would be added to us.

'For we are but of yesterday, and know nothing, because our days upon earth are a shadow' (Job 8:9).

'For man also knoweth not his time: as the fishes that are taken in an evil net, and as the birds that are caught in the snare; so are the sons of men snared in an evil time, when it falleth suddenly upon them' (Ecclesiastes 9:12).

'Cast thy bread upon the waters: for thou shalt find it after many days. Give a portion to seven, and also to eight; for thou knowest not what evil shall be upon the earth. If the clouds be full of rain, they empty themselves upon the earth: and if the tree fall toward the south, or toward the north, in the place where the tree falleth, there it shall be. He that observeth the wind shall not sow; and he that regardeth the clouds shall not reap. As thou knowest not what is the way of the spirit, nor how the bones do grow in the womb of her that is with child: even so thou knowest not the works of God who maketh all' (Ecclesiastes 11:1-5).

Man has limited knowledge of his needs on earth. Many think they need pleasure, money and other things but God revealed man's real need in the Bible. The Scriptures declared that man's days on earth are a shadow. For what purpose then do men fiercely pursue earthly things without knowing God's mind first? This is an important question, for God alone has the divine timetable of every man's life on earth.

It is possible to zealously pursue goals and achieve them. However, no goal outside the will of God can accomplish your purpose on earth. When you avoid God to pursue other things, it is so easy for devil to capture you and unleash his own agenda for your life. Satan can re-draw the map of your life and lead you into deadly errors.

> *'The fear of the Lord is the beginning of knowledge: but fools despise wisdom and instruction'* (<u>Proverbs 1:7</u>)

> *'The way of peace they know not; and there is no judgment in their goings: they have made them crooked paths: whosoever goeth therein shall not know peace'* (<u>Isaiah 59:8</u>)

> *'Therefore I said, Surely these are poor; they are foolish: for they know not the way of the Lord, nor the judgment of their God'* (<u>Jeremiah 5:4</u>)

There is God's presence on earth. Satan also has his presence on earth. When you ignore God, it becomes easy for the devil to deceive you and become your master. So many people have rushed into things of this world, including marriages without seeking God. Moreover, once in error, they remain stuck, not knowing how long their problems will last because God was never in their plans.

In midst of trouble, people who do not trust God end up as fishes catch in an evil net or birds caught in snare. Such people, when married and in trouble, settle for a lifetime of confusion. We must always trust God, commit our ways into His hands and wait for His divine direction. You do not know the way of the Spirit, or how growth takes place in the womb. Likewise, we have no idea of God's will and plan until He shows us. Jesus came to show us the only way to God and we must respond.

> *'Come unto me, all ye that labor and are heavy laden, and I will give you rest. Take my yoke upon you, and learn of me; for I am meek and lowly in heart: and ye shall find rest unto your souls. For my yoke is easy, and my burden is light'* (<u>Matthew 11:28-30</u>).

Jesus is the way of peace and He alone can lead us back to God of peace. He alone can restore peace into our broken lives and marriages. No matter how badly devil has ruined you and your marriage, Jesus can restore you and your marriage to original.

> *'He was in the world, and the world was made by him, and the world knew him not'* (<u>John 1:10</u>).

> *'Jesus answered and said unto her, If thou knewest the gift of God, and who it is that saith to thee, Give me to drink; thou wouldest have asked of him, and he would have given thee living water'* (<u>John 4:10</u>).

'Jesus said unto them, If ye were blind, ye should have no sin: but now ye say, We see; therefore your sin remaineth' (Revelation 3:17).

Jesus was before the universe came into being. He made the world. No one can change this or succeed on earth without Jesus. Everyone has erred and needs Christ for his or her sins to be forgiven. Humble and surrender yourself, and your sins will be forgiven. Christ is God's gift to man and without Him no one will get to God. You cannot have peace in your marriage when you refuse to drink the water of life, which is Christ.

Chapter 2

THERE IS NO MORE WINE

So many people have shut Christ out of the early days of their marriages because of premarital immoral acts. If you break the spiritual and ordained law of God in marriage, the wine of your marriage will finish so soon.

'And he answered and said unto them, Have ye not read, that he which made them at the beginning made them male and female, And said, For this cause shall a man leave father and mother, and shall cleave to his wife: and they twain shall be one flesh? Wherefore they are no more twain, but one flesh. What therefore God

hath joined together, let not man put asunder'
(Matthew 19:4-6).

If you have married and yet nurturing plans to marry the second time when your first legally married partner still lives, Jesus cannot bless your wedding. That second marriage is illegal because God made them male and female.

You may have enough wealth in your possession to invite the best of dignitaries in the whole world. You may satisfy everyone with wine and even get them intoxicated. Eventually, the wine of your marriage will finish and your marriage will lack ingredients that keep marriages happy. If you pull down what God has put together, your marriage will not succeed.

> *'Marriage is honorable in all, and the bed undefiled: but whoremongers and adulterers God will judge'*
> (Hebrews 13:4).

God made marriage to be honorable. When you are married and still engage in adulterous affairs, you are defiling your bed and God promised to judge all adulterers. You may not see the judgment now but eventually, your marriage wine will finish. If you enter in the house of God and begin to commit immorality, you are drinking your marriage wine in sin. When you get pregnant or get someone impregnated, you despise God's name. If you sleep with someone's daughter without marriage, you are drinking the wine of marriage without permission. It is sinful to do that. You are blaspheming the name of God and breaking a holy tradition. If you marry without your parent's consent, you break God's law.

'Thou shalt not remove thy neighbor's landmark, which they of old time have set in thine inheritance, which thou shalt inherit in the land that the Lord thy God giveth thee to possess it' (<u>Deuteronomy 19:14</u>).

'Cursed be he that removeth his neighbor's landmark. And all the people shall say, Amen' (<u>Deuteronomy 27:17</u>).

Marriage is an ancient trademark and should not be done without God's consent. If you remove your neighbor's landmark, you get a curse. If you enter any church, they will have a tradition and a way of marriage. In every community and tribe, there is a way of marriage. This must be observed according to God's Word. You are expected to observe all the traditions, except that which is contrary to faith and pure conscience. Where God's authority is made plain, the traditions or church customs bow and cease. No church or family custom ought to require anything that contradicts God's Word in marriage.

'But Peter and John answered and said unto them, Whether it be right in the sight of God to hearken unto you more than unto God, judge ye' (<u>Acts 4:19</u>).

'Then Peter and the other apostles answered and said, We ought to obey God rather than men' (<u>Acts 5:29</u>).

You need the consent of your parents and the church to do the right thing before it is accepted by God. Anything that is worth doing is worth doing very well. The reasons why marriage's wine dries up in many families too early are numerous. If you marry someone who is not compatible both in faith and in some other areas, your marriage wine may finish before time.

> 'Neither shalt thou make marriages with them; thy daughter thou shalt not give unto his son, nor his daughter shalt thou take unto thy son' (Deuteronomy 7:3).

> 'Be ye not unequally yoked together with unbelievers: for what fellowship hath righteousness with unrighteousness? And what communion hath light with darkness?' (2 Corinthians 6:14).

Not every member of same community is marriageable at a time. It could even be worse to marry outside your religion without God's leading. You need God's leading to marry the most intelligent or most beautiful and religious persons. They may be good for other persons but not actually good for you. God knows who is best fitting for you. So, when you rush to make a choice for yourself, your marriage wine will finish before your expectation.

More so, it is bad to marry someone who is an unbeliever. This is because two cannot walk together if they do not agree. Moreover, if at first you disagreed, it will be wise to find ways to agree for there is and will be no room for divorce in God's New Testament book. Sex outside marriage, or living as husband and wife before marriage will be a satanic way of consummating. It is having a fellowship with the unfruitful works of darkness. All these can cause the wine in marriage to expire so soon.

'And have no fellowship with the unfruitful works of darkness, but rather reprove them. For it is a shame even to speak of those things which are done of them in secret' (<u>Ephesians 5:11-12</u>).

'For he that biddeth him God speed is partaker of his evil deeds' (<u>2 John 1:11</u>).

This kind of life can bring shame into families and cause marriage wine to finish. Any marriage that starts with sin and disobedience to God's Word will suffer.

THINGS THAT CAN CAUSE WINE TO FINISH

- *Eating the forbidden fruit of marriage.*

- *Going down to Egypt to beg for bread in times of family problems or seeking help from outside God when problems come into the family.*

- *Being impatient to wait for God's visitation in times of satanic attacks or delays. (See Genesis 16:1-21)*

- *Being wicked to people.*

- *Despising your birthright and cheating in marriage (adultery).*

- *Complaining in times of problems instead of praying and waiting for God's time of manifestation.*

- *Marring the wrong person and trying to solve your problems your own way outside God's way*

- *Having many women outside your marriage or many men outside your marriage (See 1 Kings 11:1-19).*

- *Fighting people who tells you the truth (See Matthew 14:1-13, Mark 6:17-28).*

- *Bewitching others and practicing witchcraft (See Acts 8:9-13, 18-24).*

- *Shedding innocent blood (See Acts 12:1-9, 20-25, 2 Samuel 21:1-9).*

WHAT HAPPENS WHEN THE WINE IS FINISHED?

- *When the wine is finished, Satan will invade homes and families.*

- *There will be presence of anti-marriage forces in homes.*

- *There may be strange men or women coming in (Jezebels and Delilah's).*

- *Evil interference of in-laws and unfriendly friends multiplies.*

- *There will be home manipulators' presence. Conflicts and hostilities will set in.*

- *God's original map or His plans for the marriages will be re-drawn by the devil.*

- *Bondages will increase and hatred will take over. There will be communication gaps, foolishness and unprofitable compromises.*

- *There will be partial separation (incomplete leaving and incomplete cleaving).*

- *There may be open sin, adultery, lack of submission, love and selfishness.*

- *There will be renewal of unconscious links to ancient covenants and renewal of inherited curses, and return to parental families to bring the consequences of collective captivity of evil family pattern.*

- *Families will be demonized with the returning of familiar spirit attacks in dreams, sex in dreams, and many other dream attacks.*

- *A whole family will begin to suffer. Father, mother and if they have children, will suffer even more.*

- *There will be an increase of bitterness, rejection, depression, fears, and worry etc.*

- *Unforgiving spirits, compromise of faith, confusion and all kinds of problems will surface; even pre-mature deaths, leaving the children to suffer.*

DELIVERANCE FOR FAMILIES IN TROUBLE

People take different directions when their marriage gets into trouble. Some separate, divorce or marry other wives. God who knows everything knows that at some point in time, in this world, the wine of some marriages will get finished. Therefore, He made a way of escape from marital troubles, and this is not separation, divorce or marrying another person. So when you find out that your marriage wine has finished, invite Christ back to your marriage to increase the wine.

> 'And the third day there was a marriage in Cana of Galilee; and the mother of Jesus was there' (John 2:1).

> 'And one of the Pharisees desired him that he would eat with him. And he went into the Pharisee's house, and sat down to meat. And, behold, a woman in the city, which was a sinner, when she knew that Jesus sat at meat in the Pharisee's house, brought an alabaster box of ointment, And stood at his feet behind him weeping, and began to wash his feet with tears, and did wipe them with the hairs of her head, and kissed his feet, and anointed them with the ointment. Now when the Pharisee which had bidden him saw it, he spake within himself, saying, This man, if he were a prophet, would have known who and what manner of woman this is that toucheth him: for she is a sinner. And Jesus answering said unto him, Simon, I have somewhat to say unto thee. And he saith, Master, say on. There was a certain creditor, which had two debtors: the one owed five hundred pence, and the other fifty. And when they had nothing to pay, he frankly forgave them both. Tell me therefore, which of

them will love him most? Simon answered and said, I suppose that he, to whom he forgave most. And he said unto him, Thou hast rightly judged. And he turned to the woman, and said unto Simon, Seest thou this woman? I entered into thine house, thou gavest me no water for my feet: but she hath washed my feet with tears, and wiped them with the hairs of her head. Thou gavest me no kiss: but this woman since the time I came in hath not ceased to kiss my feet. My head with oil thou didst not anoint: but this woman hath anointed my feet with ointment. Wherefore I say unto thee, Her sins, which are many, are forgiven; for she loved much: but to whom little is forgiven, the same loveth little. And he said unto her, Thy sins are forgiven. And they that sat at meat with him began to say within themselves, Who is this that forgiveth sins also? And he said to the woman, Thy faith hath saved thee; go in peace' (Luke 7:36-50).

If only you can acknowledge your sins, repent of them and forsake them, Christ will come back to your family and restore it. When the Pharisee invited Jesus into his house, Jesus went to the house. No matter how sinful or how bad the trouble in your family is, Jesus can honor your invitation. Mary Magdalene was one of the worst sinners of her time but Jesus delivered her and she made it. If you will truly repent, Jesus will bring His new wine into your marriage and the whole situation will improve.

'And when they wanted wine, the mother of Jesus saith unto him, They have no wine' (John 2:3-10).

Jesus is always ready to perform miracles in your marriage. He will bring peace, joy and happiness that you need and everyone will see it and testify. In a home where there is wine from Jesus, the wife is always spiritual, meek, quiet, humble, obedient, and submissive in everything. She does not oppose God's Word. She is quiet, loving, diligent, hospitable, prayerful, and a true mother and dependable. The husband in a family with wine from Jesus always plans how to provide for the family. He teaches, guides, leads, prays and provides for the whole family. As the head, he stays and leads the body.

> 'So ought men to love their wives as their own bodies. He that loveth his wife loveth himself. For no man ever yet hated his own flesh; but nourisheth and cherisheth it, even as the Lord the church: For we are members of his body, of his flesh, and of his bones. For this cause shall a man leave his father and mother, and shall be joined unto his wife, and they two shall be one flesh. This is a great mystery: but I speak concerning Christ and the church. Nevertheless let every one of you in particular so love his wife even as himself; and the wife see that she reverence her husband' (Ephesians 5:28-33).

He loves his wife not because of what he can get from her but because it is a commandment from God.

Intervention of Jesus in Godly Homes: The family that invites Jesus into their house may have worldly problems, but these problems will not last or destroy the family. Once, they pray, Christ answers.

Examples of God's Interventions: God visited Adam and Eve the day the serpent tricked them in the garden. If Adam and Eve had told God the truth, they would have been delivered. If you have an evil visitor in your home, you can cry out to God. The purpose of this book is to encourage you to cry out to God. If you pray, God will visit you and deliver you. He will bring his wine into your family. No one has ever sincerely cried to God and He failed to respond.

- *Abel cried to God and He answered.*

- *Noah obeyed God and cried for salvation, God provided an ark and saved his family from mass destruction*

- *Abraham cried for Sodom and Gomorrah and God delivered Lot.*

- *Ishmael cried and God delivered him and provided for him*

- *(See Genesis 21:1-21).*

- *Jacob cried and God showed him a way to heaven. He cried again, and his name was changed.*

- *Leah cried and God opened her womb (See Genesis 29:35-30).*

- *Rachael cried and God opened her womb (See Genesis 30:22-24).*

- *Abraham cried and his wife conceived at the old age and she gave birth to a baby boy.*

- *The children of Israel cried out in their bondage, and God called Moses to deliver them from Pharaoh.*

- *Moses cried and God provided food for His people. He received a law to guide his people.*

- *Joshua cried and he received power to stop the moon and the sun for a whole day.*

- *Gideon cried and God empowered him to deliver his people.*

- *Samson cried and the children of philistines were avenged.*

- *Hannah cried and she received a godly child that served his generation.*

- *David cried and he recovered his lost family (See 1 Samuel 30:1-32).*

- *Elijah cried and God used him to bring rain in Israel.*

- *Elisha cried and received double portion.*

- *Hezekiah cried and God delivered him from premature death.*

- *Jabez cried and God enlarged his coast.*

- *Daniel cried and he was delivered from the den of lions.*

- *Esther and Mordecai cried and the evil decree against their family was reversed.*

If you can cry, God will visit your family with a wine from heaven. Peace can be restored to your family. You can enjoy your marriage again and God can remove every trouble. What you need to do is to repent and forsake your sins.

Once you repent, you can then pray and God will dine with you in your family today. Forgive all that offended you, especially all that are in your house. Your wife, your husband, children and all that offended you. Ask for forgiveness where you need to ask. Then take time to pray the prayers in this book.

You have every reason to -

- *Drive away the serpent in the garden of your family.*

- *Invite Christ into your home once again and ask him to reign and rule forever.*

- *Ask Jesus to remove all troubles from your home, the ones you or others invited.*

- *Uproot the pillar of witchcraft in your family.*

- *Use God's anointing to destroy every problem in your family.*

- *Destroy all the works of devil in your family.*

- *Ask God to deliver you and everyone in your family.*

- *Disconnect from all evil connections in your family.*

- *Build back the bridges you have destroyed.*

- *Frustrate the works of witchcraft in your family.*

- *Chase away every stranger in your homes.*

- *Trouble your troubles unto death.*

Chapter 3

CONVERSION AND ASSURANCE OF SALVATION

Before you go further, I advise you first ensure you are converted and saved. It will not be of much good to pray without hope for earthly and eternal results. Many people rush into prayers and start their Christian lives without first ensuring conversion and salvation. It is wrong and that is why many are having problems in their Christian lives today, and praying many prayers without results.

God wants you to have assurance that you are saved or born again after receiving Jesus as your personal Lord and Savior before praying for other blessings in life. Many have been deceived into believing that in mastering the art of prayer, they can receive blessings and enjoy them without assurance of salvation.

> 'He came unto his own, and his own received him not. But as many as received him, to them gave he power to become the sons of God, even to them that believe on his name' (*John 1:11-12*).

> 'He that turneth away his ear from hearing the law, even his prayer shall be abomination' (*Proverb 28:9*).

It is a deceit to jump into prayers without conversion and assurance of salvation.

WHAT IS CONVERSION?

Conversion is the turning away of a sinner from his or her former ways to God's ways, and asking for forgiveness of sins. Sinners who turn away from their sins and turn to Christ in righteousness are said to be converted. Jesus told Peter to strengthen his brethren when he is converted.

When someone is converted, his or her sins are blotted out, qualifying him or her to pray for other blessings from God that can make him rich without adding any sorrow. It is possible to receive answers to your prayers without conversion, but sorrows will eventually trail your blessings.

Peter advised the people to be converted first so that their sins will be blotted out, to enable them to appear in God's presence in times of prayer. Even after being saved, when you err from the truth and repent, your prayers will be answered.

> 'Brethren, if any of you do err from the truth, and one convert him; Let him know, that he which converteth the sinner from the error of his way shall save a soul from death, and shall hide a multitude of sins' (James 5:19-20).

Another important thing before you repent or confess your sins and pray is that you must be prepared and determined to forsake your sins because God cannot be deceived into believing that you are a genuine convert.

> 'And now also the axe is laid unto the root of the trees: every tree therefore which bringeth not forth good fruit is hewn down, and cast into the fire.

And the people asked him, saying, What shall we do then? He answereth and saith unto them, He that hath two coats, let him impart to him that hath none; and he that hath meat, let him do likewise. Then came also publicans to be baptized, and said unto him, Master, what shall we do? And he said unto them, Exact no more than that which is appointed you. And the soldiers likewise demanded of him, saying, And what shall we do? And he said unto them, Do violence to no man, neither accuse any falsely; and be content with your wages' (Luke 3:9-14).

Take time to search your heart and see if you are really determined to forsake and detest the sins you are about to confess and denounce before God. This is very important. Many people are always ready to rush to the altar for altar calls to confess their sins, but they have not taken some time to determine first in their hearts if they are truly ready to forsake their sins and repent.

Do not rush into confession of sins you are not determined to forsake. God may not answer your prayers. He already knows that you are only confessing and will not forsake your sins. Likewise, when you have an alternative to God, He is not under any obligation to answer your prayers. If you want to keep sinning and think you can just tell God lies, and ask Him for blessings, you may not be answered.

If you receive any answer at all, it will likely be from the devil in order to lure and capture your soul. I want to tell you the truth so that the truth can set you free. The devil may allow you to get answers to your prayers from him once he knows you are not ready to stop the sins you are confessing to God.

The devil is the source and supplier of all answers, prosperity, and health when you are enjoying in your sins, and not God. So do not be deceived.

> 'Be not deceived; God is not mocked: for whatsoever a man soweth, that shall he also reap. For he that soweth to his flesh shall of the flesh reap corruption; but he that soweth to the Spirit shall of the Spirit reap life everlasting' (Galatians 6:7-8).

> 'And when Saul inquired of the Lord, the Lord answered him not, neither by dreams nor by Urim, nor by prophets. Then said Saul unto his servants, Seek me a woman that hath a familiar spirit, that I may go to her, and inquire of her. And his servants said to him, Behold, there is a woman that hath a familiar spirit at Endor' (1 Samuel 28:6-7).

If you have in mind to consult other powers while you pray to God, He may not answer you. God knows what is in your mind no matter the quantity of prayers you pray. Sincerity of heart before God during prayers is one of the vital requirements for your prayers to be answered.

Some answers that sinners receive when they pray with deceitful minds are not from God but from the devil. It is better not to receive answers for your prayers at all than to receive it from the devil. When devil blesses anyone, that person will use his or her whole life to pay the devil back.

Any answer to prayers or blessings from the devil is useless and as painful as death. Many people are already deceived into these types of blessings and answers. However, you can be converted if you desire for the truth that can set you free.

> 'And ye shall know the truth, and the truth shall make you free. If the Son therefore shall make you free, ye shall be free indeed' (John 8:32, 36).

In the midst of delays to your prayers, you must wait for God and be prepared to identify yourself as Christ's disciple, and resolutely fight forever under His banner until victory comes. God wants us to remain humble but confident. When you trust Christ, your sins are forgiven and victory is sure, regardless of the circumstances ahead or now. Our hope is that those who turn to Jesus Christ are already accepted and will find their sins forgiven with blessings of all kinds attached.

The death of Jesus has made a full, perfect and sufficient sacrifice for the sins of the whole world, while waiting for truly repentant sinners to come and partake.

> 'When Jesus therefore had received the vinegar, he said, It is finished: and he bowed his head, and gave up the ghost' (John 19:30).

> 'For if the blood of bulls and of goats, and the ashes of an heifer sprinkling the unclean, sanctifieth to the purifying of the flesh: How

much more shall the blood of Christ, who through the eternal Spirit offered himself without spot to God, purge your conscience from dead works to serve the living God?' (Hebrews 9:13-14).

Jesus suffered on our behalf, bowed down his head and gave up the ghost for you to rise forever. His blood is able to provide all manner of blessings for those who will confess and are ready to forsake their sins. All is finished and nothing remains but man's acceptance of gains of Calvary. If you are a backslider, you need to return to God.

'My little children, these things write I unto you, that ye sin not. And if any man sin, we have an advocate with the Father, Jesus Christ the righteous: And he is the propitiation for our sins: and not for ours only, but also for the sins of the whole world' (1 John 2:1-2).

'Wherefore lay apart all filthiness and superfluity of naughtiness, and receive with meekness the engrafted word, which is able to save your souls' (James 1:21)

If you are a sinner, you do not need to remain in sin. Repent and forsake your sins and your prayers will be answered.

'But the fruit of the Spirit is love, joy, peace, longsuffering, gentleness, goodness, faith, Meekness, temperance: against such there is no law. And they that are Christ's have crucified the flesh with the affections and lusts. If we live in the

Spirit, let us also walk in the Spirit. Let us not be desirous of vain glory, provoking one another, envying one another' (<u>Galatians 5:22-26</u>).

EVIDENCE OF TRUE CONVERSION

A truly converted person will show evidence of conversion and reconciliation by living a Christ-like life. With the enmity removed and the wall of separation broken down, he is henceforth at peace with God. He has peace within himself and he is free from condemnation. He is no longer separated from God and he can know and recognize when God's presence manifests. He has stripped off the filthy rags of the old self and put on the robes of holiness. His life is changed and will reflect a true Christian's life.

As a child resembles his parents, so does a Christian resemble Christ who saved him or her from all sins. The peace of God and other fruits of the Spirit, when abundant in our hearts will overcome, extinguish and put down all evil desires, agitations and uprising in the heart and enthrone Christ. The love of God overthrows every fake love or lusts and makes a Christian to love God above all things.

Any Christian locked into God's love puts God first in all things in life. Such a one loves God and fellow humans sincerely from the heart. He or she does not put personal interests or way of life first, like most people in the world. He or she does not regard ambitions or goals of earthly life above blessings that agree with eternal life, but is soundly converted and called out from the evil activities of the world. He is a born again child of God, having his heart regenerated and transformed.

> *'Then will I sprinkle clean water upon you, and ye shall be clean: from all your filthiness, and from all your idols, will I cleanse you. A new heart also will I give you, and a new spirit will I put within*

you: and I will take away the stony heart out of your flesh, and I will give you a heart of flesh. And I will put my spirit within you, and cause you to walk in my statutes, and ye shall keep my judgments, and do them' (<u>Ezekiel 36:25-27</u>).

Such a person walks daily in the light of the Word of God, which he or she has received, having no desire any longer to live for self but for God. He or she hates the world and loves God's perfect kingdom. He or she does not yield to lusts of the flesh and eyes, or covetousness and all kinds of evil in the world.

The world, which we refer to here, is not the entirety of God's universe, and all humans inhabiting the earth. The world we are referring to are societies organized without reference to God. We must hate things that make people proud or to pursue godless power and positions without God, and self-righteousness together with beauty and riches without Christ.

Anything in the world that attracts sin, evil or open rebellion against the written Word of God must be rejected.

PURITY OF HEART BEFORE PRAYER

It is wise to meet God's requirement on purity before going to Him in prayer. Heart purity is God's demand from his children. For a Christian to attain this level, he or she is expected to do some needful things. It is very important because those who have this experience enjoy their marriages, overcome all troubles while on earth and live with God eternally in heaven.

I want you to believe God for all you are going to ask Him, for having asked, He will answer your prayers.

> *'Who shall ascend into the hill of the Lord? Or who shall stand in his holy place? He that hath clean hands, and a pure heart; who hath not lifted up his soul unto vanity, nor sworn deceitfully'* (*Psalm 24:3-4*).

> *'Now the end of the commandment is charity out of a pure heart, and of a good conscience, and of faith unfeigned'* (*1 Timothy 1:5*).

> *'Follow peace with all men, and holiness, without which no man shall see the Lord'* (*Hebrews 12:14*).

With holiness and good prayer life, you can get (*ascend*) into heaven, the hill of the Lord, to seek your rightful partner, and keep your marriage to the end without threats of separation and divorce, maintaining a lasting joy and happiness in your marriage.

With holiness experience, you can overcome all earthly vanities, and live like a king or queen, loving your partner with a pure heart and good conscience, with assurance of making heaven with all members of your family. This experience will help you to keep your family in peace, pursuing peace with all men.

Holiness is very important for those who have it enjoy God's goodness and power in their lives.

> *'Jesus answered and said unto him, Verily, verily, I say unto thee, Except a man be born again, he cannot see the kingdom of God' (John 3:3).*

> *'And the brethren immediately sent away Paul and Silas by night unto Berea: who coming thither went into the synagogue of the Jews' (Acts 17:10).*

> *'He that covereth his sins shall not prosper: but whoso confesseth and forsaketh them shall have mercy' (Proverb 28:13).*

> *'If we say that we have no sin, we deceive ourselves, and the truth is not in us' (1 John 1:8).*

Nicodemus was a Pharisee who attended Jewish worship regularly and did good works. He must have been paying his tithes too, praying, fasting and doing all other religious things. He earned respect and recognition among the Jews, yet Jesus revealed to him the greatest and most important need in his life. He needed to be born again.

Being born again is a step you have to take first before you think of heart purity and living a holy life. This experience is very essential for the first birth was sin. As a result of all the sins that men have committed, at least once in their lives, no one can go to heaven without being born gain. Immediately the new birth takes place in someone's life, the sinful heart will be cleansed and renewed by the blood of Jesus Christ.

If this is not done, no one can claim to be born again, or think of having a pure heart or living a holy life, and even making heaven.

> 'Let the wicked forsake his way, and the unrighteous man his thoughts: and let him return unto the Lord, and he will have mercy upon him; and to our God, for he will abundantly pardon' (Isaiah 55:7).

> 'If we confess our sins, he is faithful and just to forgive us our sins, and to cleanse us from all unrighteousness' (1 John 1:9).

Steps To Be Born Again:

a. Recognize that you have sinned, confess all your sins and be willing to turn away from your sins.
b. Your decision must be genuine and sincere.
c. Turn away from all your evil thoughts and sinful desires.
d. Give your heart to Jesus and ask Him to control all your life.

> 'He came unto his own, and his own received him not. But as many as received him, to them gave he power to become the sons of God, even to them that believe on his name' (John 1:11-12).

33

'And he said to the woman, Thy faith hath saved thee; go in peace' (Luke 7:50).

To be sure that you are born again, you have to contend with every evil that manifests in your life and believe God's Word. Have faith in God's Word and His promises that says that He will save all who turn away from their sins and give their lives to Christ.

Refuse to give in to your feelings and believe only God's Word. As you stand firm in God's Word, you will begin to experience changes in your desires, feelings, thoughts and the changes will begin to manifest physically as long as you continue in obedience to God's Word.

A genuine obedience will make you to hate sin, love God and want to please Him more than anybody or anything else. You will no longer be attracted to the company of sinners. Rather, you will develop supernatural love and preference to be with believers attending fellowships, and even tell others about Jesus who saves from sin. Your behaviors will begin to change for the best as you resist sin and abhor all evil to live like Christ. As a new creature, you will also experience forgiveness of sin and freedom from the power of sin.

HOW TO HAVE A PURE HEART

A pure heart is one that loves holiness and righteousness. It does not condone sin but desires to be more and more holy in all areas of life. It contends to attain the level of God's love, power and to please God at all times in everything. If you want to receive this blessing, you need to surrender your will, desire and ambition to God completely.

> *'I beseech you therefore, brethren, by the mercies of God, that ye present your bodies a living sacrifice, holy, acceptable unto God, which is your reasonable service. And be not conformed to this world: but be ye transformed by the renewing of your mind, that ye may prove what is that good, and acceptable, and perfect, will of God' (Romans 12:1-2).*

> *'Blessed are they which do hunger and thirst after righteousness: for they shall be filled' (Matthew 5:6).*

> *'Therefore I say unto you, What things soever ye desire, when ye pray, believe that ye receive them, and ye shall have them' (Mark 11:24).*

Pray all prayers according to God's will. Insist on the right ways of getting anything on earth. If you pray and do not get answers for anything, wait on the Lord and do not allow worry or anxiety to distract your attention from your focus.

> *'Thus saith the Lord, Stand ye in the ways, and see, and ask for the old paths, where is the good way, and walk therein, and ye shall find rest for*

35

your souls. But they said, We will not walk therein' (Jeremiah 6:16).

'And I will wait upon the Lord, that hideth his face from the house of Jacob, and I will look for him' (Isaiah 8:17).

True believers who wish to receive direct answers to their prayers must take their stands to abide in Christ and maintain a relationship with Christ at all cost. Your relationship with Christ must be stronger and closer than any other relationship.

Your commitment to Christ must be unto death without room for compromise, negotiation or agreement. You must abide in Christ in order to reject and refuse to compromise your faith for anything on earth.

'Abide in me, and I in you. As the branch cannot bear fruit of itself, except it abide in the vine; no more can ye, except ye abide in me... If ye abide in me, and my words abide in you, ye shall ask what ye will, and it shall be done unto you...Ye have not chosen me, but I have chosen you, and ordained you, that ye should go and bring forth fruit, and that your fruit should remain: that whatsoever ye shall ask of the Father in my name, he may give it you' (John 15: 4, 7, 16).

To abide in Christ is to continue to believe in Christ, living continually in the grace and Words of Christ. The evidence of abiding in Christ is bearing Christ-like fruits that are consistent with bringing glory to God. No matter the delays, trials, distress and perplexities, you must abide in Christ.

The saints of the old persevered in faith to the end and never allowed the threats of kings, opposition of false prophets, delays to prosperity, marriages and fiery furnace, etc, to sweep off their faith. They believed God and held fast in the darkest hours when all the foundations on which men of the world built their hopes were ruthlessly swept away.

> *'I have fought a good fight, I have finished my course, I have kept the faith: Henceforth there is laid up for me a crown of righteousness, which the Lord, the righteous judge, shall give me at that day: and not to me only, but unto all them also that love his appearing'* (2 Timothy 4:7-8).

> *'Shadrach, Meshach, and Abed-nego, answered and said to the king, O Nebuchadnezzar, we are not careful to answer thee in this matter. If it be so, our God whom we serve is able to deliver us from the burning fiery furnace, and he will deliver us out of thine hand, O king. But if not, be it known unto thee, O king, that we will not serve thy gods, nor worship the golden image which thou hast set up'* (Daniel 3:16-18).

Your marriage will be preserved from divorce and separation if you handle these prayers faithfully as you repent and pray for purity of heart. In fact, whatever your problem is, if you are born again, follow the counsels in this book and prayerfully believe God, you will not regret your life on earth.

'But the fruit of the Spirit is love, joy, peace, longsuffering, gentleness, goodness, faith, Meekness, temperance: against such there is no law. And they that are Christ's have crucified the flesh with the affections and lusts. If we live in the Spirit, let us also walk in the Spirit. Let us not be desirous of vain glory, provoking one another, envying one another' (Galatians 5:22-26).

EVIDENCE OF PURE HEART

A saved and purified soul bears the fruits of the Holy Spirit. A purified soul puts God first in all things in life, despises gains that oppose God's Word and loves fellow men sincerely from heart. God's Word in such people's hearts extinguishes the fires of sin and gives no room for hatred, unforgiving spirits, envy, evil intentions towards others and pride. He loves the scriptures and rejects words that contradict it, detesting every appearance of evil, but fears only God and builds strong confidence in God's Word.

Whenever one with purified heart remembers that his or her sins are forgiven, it gives them lasting joy even in the midst of trials and problems. They have peace with God, following peace with all men. He is empowered to suffer insults, reproaches and all manners of persecution with patience. They do not compromise and go back to sin because of desires for quick blessing. They patiently trust God and pray for God's intervention.

A holy person is gentle and kind in every way. He or she is good, meek, temperate and faithful to God to the end. They trust God for the provision of every need that His promises cover. They are lowly in heart and teachable. They have self-control over their desires, tongues and appetite. Deeply rooted and grounded in love for God and others, they are always pure and they think no evil and rejoice not in iniquity. They have single eye, one mind and determination to please God both in private and in public places.

Chapter 4

THE PURPOSE OF THIS BOOK

This book is written out of compassion and burden in my heart to meet up with continuous demands from people all over the world. My heart is overwhelmed with prayer needs. Many believers who have rights to live prosperous lives are under serious demonic oppressions and many are getting confused in every passing day. As a result, I started praying and God led me to write many prayer points and books that can direct people to pray targeted prayers against different problems relating to several issues of life.

FASTING AND PRAYERS

Many people seek closer walk with God but they do not know how to pray. This prayer series is an answer to such need. Fasting is not a legalistic discipline, but should be adapted to each believer's individual purpose. You should determine the length of your fast.

You can get great result by reading this book, praying the prayers in it alone if your heart is perfectly prepared. If your heart is pure, and you add fasting to your prayers as you follow through in this book, the results will shake your foundation like a windstorm bending a sapling, and every evil structure and deposits in your life will bow. It is necessary to note that religious practices as fasting are less important than doing God's will, but if you do God's will and add fasting and prayer, all impossibilities standing before you will bow. Fasting helps to lose the bonds of wickedness, frees people from evil addictions, and undoes heavy burdens, solve problems and overcome barriers that keep people away from God's plans, promises and God's provisions. Fasting helps to let the oppressed go free, breaks evil yokes, brings in God's light, restores lost health and bring down God's glory.

> *'Is not this the fast that I have chosen? To lose the bands of wickedness, to undo the heavy burdens, and to let the oppressed go free, and that ye break every yoke? Is it not to deal thy bread to the hungry, and that thou bring the poor that are cast out to thy house? When thou seest the naked, that thou cover him; and that thou hide not thyself from thine own flesh? Then shall thy light break forth as the morning, and thine health shall spring forth*

speedily: and thy righteousness shall go before thee; the glory of the LORD shall be thy rearward' (Isaiah 58:6-8).

You can go into normal fast, which is going without food for a definite period during which you take only liquids like water or juice. The duration depends on you. It can be up to 40 days or more.

Absolute fast allows no food or water at all, while partial fast is to avoid certain foods or is on a schedule that includes limited eating. It means missing one meal in a day or eating only flesh vegetables for some time. A rational fast consists of eating or omitting certain types of food for a designated time. You may decide not to eat your favorite food or eat after few days. Jonathan Edward fasted for 22 hours prior to preaching his famous sermon *'Sinners in the hands of an angry God'*.

WHY DO WE NEED TO FAST AND PRAY?

- Because many people are under satanic attacks and many are now confused.

- Because of increase in witchcraft and occult activities

- Because many problems are beyond medical science and mysterious deaths are on the increase.

- Because many people are at cross road, hopeless and peace is scarce all over the world.

- Because of political instability and need for national healing.

- Because of unsolved family problems in many homes, the increase of divorce cases, separations and single parents in the society.

- Because of family troubles, increase in unemployment, youth violence and social unrests.

- Because of occult activities in the church and demonic attacks on believers

- Because the church and the society is in need of people of character and integrity, as many destructive bad habits have captured many people in our generation.

- Many need protection from evil forces and they are not getting it.

- Because many great people, especially believers, are entangled in economic meltdown

- Because of the debilitating and deplorable health situations of many, even in the abundance of food and medical technology in our generation

- Because of the growing number of youths who are engaged in terrorism.

- Because of the increase of wars, quest for power, fame, position and love of money among the restless and vibrant youths.

- Because evil men are increasing, and the wicked people getting richer and the number of poor people getting at its higher increase.

- Because of worldliness, pleasure, manifestation of unclean spirits and sexual demons

The reason for rampant satanic evil invasions today in the world is high level of ignorance in our Christian communities. We have lowered the effectiveness of the Christian life and comprised its standards greatly. Only few people among the professing Christians actually know the true meaning of Christianity and God's demand in many areas of life. Materialism has replaced the true faith and many are now pursuing shadows. Prayers of deliverance, fasting and prayers for revival are needed in our generation from the leadership to the last person in the church and our communities. Sin, flesh and demonstrations of carnality are on the increase.

We need to go back to the Scriptures and find out from God what is wrong. The burden in my heart as I write these books is to provide insights into various topics of great concern before prayers are offered. Many religious prayer groups and deliverance ministers have been converted to join occult groups because of famine of God's Word.

They pray without true knowledge of God and His Word, do deliverance without righteousness, command power without purity, gifts without grace, discernment without discipline, and faith without fruits. Many prayer groups, deliverance ministries are turning to evil gathering of people who perform miracles without mercy, healing without holiness.

Many leaders lack God's grace, purity, discipline, mercy, love and other fruit of the spirit, and yet they lead others. We need to know and experience the basis of truth before prayers are offered to God.

THOU SHALL NOT PRAY WITCHCRAFT PRAYERS

There are two major issues I will address here, one is the issue of decreeing 'die' word in prayers and the second is whether evil spirits die or not. It is wrong to have someone in mind when praying, with the aim of wishing secretly for that person's death. If in your prayers you wish someone to die, it is very unscriptural and a practice of witchcraft.

Many congregations, who pray having in mind to kill someone, have been led into witchcraft groups. In one of my books titled **Upon All These Prayers, I** discussed this issue in detail (I recommend the book).

Let us see what death means when we pray or say '*die*' in our prayers, as you will notice and pray in this book. We do not mean that witches, wizards or human beings should die. Spirits do not die in the way that many people think.

WHAT THEN IS DEATH?

In chapter One of my book, 'Upon All These Prayers', I wrote that death is a permanent cassation of all living things. Cassation means stop! It is decreeing a 'coming to an end' of unwanted operations of a thing existing for long, or existence of undesired or illegal occupation.

Spirits will not die, but can cease from operation. It can be stopped or diverted from particular action. Alternatively, they can be kept from operating in a particular life, place, family or nation. When you pray and the spirits behind your problems are stopped, the physical manifestation of such demonic operations would begin to disappear and vanish. This is what we refer to as *death* in our prayer.

> *'Death means the end of life. The spirit living inside you or attacking your life can die by your terminating its vital functions. They can die by your casting them out. When her actions against your life is ended by your prayers, the spirit has died or has left you and her concerned may die gradually or instantly, whichever way, as far as your life is converted, the spirit is dead. When the vital functions of a spirit is permanently terminated in the life of a particular person, thing, place, then that spirit is dead in that person, thing or place, it will cease to function. Death means separation. Physical death is the separation of the soul and spirit from the body'* (James 2:26).

Spiritual death is the separation from God (See Ephesians 2:1, 12). It means living without God in this world. When someone dies and separates from God, he still lives somewhere, though he is regarded as dead. When someone dies a physical death and separates from his loves ones, he is regarded as a dead person, though he lives on somewhere in heaven or hell. The second death is the final, permanent and eternal separation from God. (*See* <u>Revelation 20:15</u>).

When we pray and say *'die!'*, we therefore mean that spirits behind a particular problem should separate and once the spirit separates, the problem will simply lose its power and grip. My heart often bleeds when I see pastors mislead their members by teaching or allowing them to pray for the death of their fellow human beings (their perceived enemies). This kind of prayer has converted such people who practice them as witches and wizards without them knowing it. What a pity!

Many people who are dead spiritually or living in terrible sins are praying for the death of their fellow humans instead of praying for repentance. In one of the sub-headings of my book titled **Upon All These Prayers**, I made it clear that the dead cannot kill evil or death.

You cannot be dead before your creator and yet issue *'death'* commands to problems. You need a copy of 'Upon All These Prayers' to learn more. When you repent, pray right prayers and live your life according to God's Word, God will defend you. Those who are unrepentant will die whether you pray or not but know that you cannot force God to kill the worst sinner, witches or wizard who is ready to repent. God also loves them.

> *'And the Lord said unto him, Arise, and go into the street which is called Straight, and inquire in the*

house of Judas for one called Saul, of Tarsus: for, behold, he prayeth' (<u>Acts 9:11</u>).

'Seest thou how Ahab humbleth himself before me? Because he humbleth himself before me, I will not bring the evil in his days: but in his son's days will I bring the evil upon his house' (<u>1 Kings 21:29</u>).

We all know that there are people like pharaoh, Herod, and others who have reprobate minds. They are in covenant and on suicide mission to kill and are never ready to repent. However, the fact is that whether you pray for their death or not, they will die anyway.

'And when it was day, certain of the Jews banded together, and bound themselves under a curse, saying that they would neither eat nor drink till they had killed Paul. And they were more than forty, which had made this conspiracy. And they came to the chief priests and elders, and said, We have bound ourselves under a great curse, that we will eat nothing until we have slain Paul' (<u>Acts 23:12-14</u>).

No matter how wicked your enemy is, if he is ready to humble himself in repentance and carry on God's assignment for his or her life, your *'fire'* and aggressive prayers cannot kill him, even when you embark on a hundred days dry fast. The only thing your prayer can do is to press your enemy to the wall. However, he has the choice to repent and live for God and make heaven.

'Manasseh was twelve years old when he began to reign, and he reigned fifty and five years in

Jerusalem: But did that which was evil in the sight of the LORD, like unto the abominations of the heathen, whom the LORD had cast out before the children of Israel. For he built again the high places which Hezekiah his father had broken down, and he reared up altars for Baalim, and made groves, and worshipped all the host of heaven, and served them' (2 Chronicles 33:1-3).

Some prayers can blind Paul and knock him down, disgrace Ahab, take Manasseh among the thorns, bind with fetters and carry him to Babylon but if he humbles himself before God and pray to the Lord, he will be delivered. Therefore, as you pray all manner of prayers, resist the devil, his agents and their influences through your prayers. If the devil's agents flee from God's wrath, they will live but if they keep to devil, they must surely die. Therefore, what do we do, to pray 'die' or not? The choice is yours.

AN EYE FOR EYE AND TOOTH FOR TOOTH

The 'An eye for an eye and tooth for tooth' law was given to Moses. It was not intended to promote or support retaliation against enemies or offenders but to guide the judges. The judges of those days were so wicked that when a person broke someone's tooth, the judges removed the entire teeth from the offender's mouth. It was to forbid the wicked judges from exacting penalties greater than the actual offence. (See Matthew 5:38-42, Exodus 21:22-25, Leviticus 24:17-22, Deuteronomy 19:15-21). The Law of Moses is good but the law of Christ is better. The law of Christ is love.

- Love God - (*See* Matthew 22:37, Psalm 122:1, 42:1-2, 2 John 6).
- Love God's Word - (*See* Jeremiah 15:16, Colossians 3:16, Psalms 1:2, 119:16, 33:72, 97, Matthew 4:4).
- Love fellow believers - (*See* John 13:34-35, 15:12, 1 John 3:16-18).
- Love sinners - (*See* John 3:16, 2 Peter 3:9, Luke 19:10, 41-44).
- Love your enemies – (*See* 1 Samuel 26:7-8, 12-25, Matthew 5:44-48, Proverb 25:21-22).

If you love your enemies, you will wish them well, pray for their conversion, even by any means necessary, so that Christ is revealed to them. It will be better for their souls to be saved than dying physically without Christ.

We must show mercy, help the poor, lend to and support the needy, but we must not give them anything that will take them away from Christ. You must not give money to people to get drunk, purchase hard drugs or commit any kind of evil.

Our responsibilities of love are:

1.   To bear each other's burden - (*See* Galatians 6:2).

2.   Greet one another - (*See* 1 Peter 5:14, Romans 16:16).

3.   Consider one another - (*See* Hebrews 10:24).

4.   Teach one another - (*See* Colossians 3:6).

5.   Edify one another - (*See* Romans 14:19, 1 Thessalonians 5:11).

6.   Comfort one another - (*See* 1 Thessalonians 4:18).

7.   Show hospitality to one to another - (*See* 1 Peter 4:9).

8.   Prefer one another to oneself - (*See* Romans 12:10).

9.   Exhort one anther - (*See* Hebrews 3:13, 10:25).

10. Minister to one another - (*See* 1 Peter 4:10).

11. Forbear one another - (*See* Colossians 3:13, Ephesians 4:32).

12. Admonish one another - (*See* Romans 12:10).

13. Forgive one another - (*See* Colossians 3:13, Ephesians 4:32).

14. Pray for one another - (*See* James 5:16).

'It is true that you may not know the details of prayers to pray for your enemy but you can pray for

their salvation. Pray that whatsoever will happen that will bring their salvation should happen. Death cannot bring their salvation but another thing may do so' (<u>Acts 8:9-24</u>).

'But Elymas the sorcerer (for so is his name by interpretation) withstood them, seeking to turn away the deputy from the faith. Then Saul, (who also is called Paul,) filled with the Holy Ghost, set his eyes on him, And said, O full of all subtilty and all mischief, thou child of the devil, thou enemy of all righteousness, wilt thou not cease to pervert the right ways of the Lord? And now, behold, the hand of the Lord is upon thee, and thou shalt be blind, not seeing the sun for a season. And immediately there fell on him a mist and a darkness; and he went about seeking some to lead him by the hand. Then the deputy, when he saw what was done, believed, being astonished at the doctrine of the Lord' (<u>Acts 13:8-12</u>).

Is it good to pray like this?

'Whosoever must die for my breakthrough to come, what are you waiting for? Die!'

'O Lord, if you must retire, sack or transfer anyone for me to keep my job, or get a job, do it'

I leave that question for each individual Christian to answer. You need to search the scripture to know the prayers to pray for all categories of people and for yourself.

However, every prayer must not remove or add to God's already written Word.

> *'For I testify unto every man that heareth the words of the prophecy of this book, If any man shall add unto these things, God shall add unto him the plagues that are written in this book: And if any man shall take away from the words of the book of this prophecy, God shall take away his part out of the book of life, and out of the holy city, and from the things which are written in this book'* (Revelation 22:18-19).

Jesus came not to condemn, but to convince, convict and convert. (*See* John 3:17, 8:11, Matthew 5:20-32, John 7:6-7, 8:44, Luke 5:8, 7:37-38, 48, 50, 8:7-9, 3:17, Matthew 18:3, James 15:19-20, Acts 3:19).

Do not say a word of prayer until you are sure that God's Word is backing those statements. God is ready to answer every prayer when His Word backs it. If you are a sincere Christian, the prayers here in this book will produce immediate answers and results.

These prayers are not ordinary. It is for believers who are determined to experience great changes. They are not easy to come by anyhow. Each prayer point is connected with immediate answers because, they are smuggled into this world across satanic check points in the heavenlies, just like the American soldiers entered Pakistan and killed Osama without normal protocol or negotiation.

'Then said He unto me, Fear not, Daniel: for from the first day that thou didst set thine heart to understand and to chasten thyself before thy God, thy words were heard, and I am come for thy words. But the prince of the kingdom of Persia withstood me one and twenty days: but, lo, Michael, one of the chief princes, came to help me; and I remained there with the kings of Persia' (Daniel 10:12-13).

They are coming directly undefiled with divine potency to deliver the oppressed, bind up the broken hearted, proclaim liberty to the captives and open the prison doors to them that are bound.

DISCOVER YOURSELF

A single prayer point in this prayer book can solve your problem. You may not need to pray for many days but there is nothing wrong to continue to pray until the answers come. Some people have a deeper and more entrenched problems and hard foundation. Our levels of bondages are not the same. We were not brought up in the same way. Our parents and places we are born are not the same. The prayer point that will set you free may not be the one that will set another person free.

> *'And he spake many things unto them in parables, saying, Behold, a sower went forth to sow; And when he sowed, some seeds fell by the way side, and the fowls came and devoured them up: Some fell upon stony places, where they had not much earth: and forthwith they sprung up, because they had no deepness of earth: And when the sun was up, they were scorched; and because they had no root, they withered away. And some fell among thorns; and the thorns sprung up, and choked them: But other fell into good ground, and brought forth fruit, some a hundredfold, some sixtyfold, some thirtyfold'* (Matthew 13:3-8).*

If you are sown (which can also mean born by the way side, or the place you were born), you will need to pray harder to be vomited by the fowls that devour people's destiny while they are alive. If you are born in a stony place, you may need to contend with the powers that scorch people's destiny. If you fall among thorns that choke people's destiny, you may need to press a little harder. Even when you are born by Christian and godly parents, you still need to fight to get at least a pass mark. For these reasons, I have prepared prayer points that you can adopt for a personal prayer program, and force your enemies to bow.

> 'Now Elisha was fallen sick of his sickness whereof he died. And Joash the king of Israel came down unto him, and wept over his face, and said, O my father, my father, the chariot of Israel, and the horsemen thereof. And Elisha said unto him, Take bow and arrows. And he took unto him bow and arrows. And he said to the king of Israel, Put thine hand upon the bow. And he put his hand upon it: and Elisha put his hands upon the king's hands. And he said, Open the window eastward. And he opened it. Then Elisha said, Shoot. And he shot. And he said, The arrow of the LORD's deliverance, and the arrow of deliverance from Syria: for thou shalt smite the Syrians in Aphek, till thou have consumed them. And he said, Take the arrows. And he took them. And he said unto the king of Israel, Smite upon the ground. And he smote thrice, and stayed. And the man of God was wroth with him, and said, Thou shouldest have smitten five or six times; then hadst thou smitten Syria till thou hadst consumed it: whereas now thou shalt smite Syria but thrice' (2 Kings 13:14-19).

If you go into a one-day program, your problem can be solved. However, you may need to pray for more days maybe three, five, seven etc. This is because a one-day program may just open the door for you to enter into your blessings. The more days you pray, the more open doors you will have and more territories you will recapture from the enemies of your destiny.

> *'Call unto me, and I will answer thee, and shew thee great and mighty things, which thou knowest not'* (Jeremiah 33:3).

> *'When a strong man armed keepeth his palace, his goods are in peace: But when a stronger than he shall come upon him, and overcome him, he taketh from him all his armor wherein he trusted, and divideth his spoils'* (Luke 11:21-22).

I encourage you to go into as many days' prayers and fasting as you can observe. Some evil spirits behind most difficult problems may not give up until you confront them with fasting and prayers. You can separate yourself, set time apart, and shun every other activity to seek the face of the Lord for days. You can also handle these prayers while attending to your official duties. However, you must set time apart at night and pray very well. The Spirit of God inspired me to write these prayers to guide you. When you fail to resist the devil, he cannot let you go just like that.

> *'And they said unto him, Thus saith Hezekiah, This day is a day of trouble, and of rebuke, and of blasphemy: for the children are come to the birth, and there is not strength to bring forth'* (Isaiah 37:3).

Many people want to enter into new things, places but they cannot. The prayers in this book are meant to take people to another level, break economic crunches, and destroy distresses and confusion in life, decree against the activities of occultism, idolatry, wickedness, spiritual weakness, discouragement, troubles, suffering, demonic violence, crisis, and powers against right decisions in life. It is meant for people of God who have lost hopes, whose reasons can no longer carry them through or people under the wrath of God.

A CHALLENGE TO PRAY

Moses went to the mountain and prayed until God gave him a law that will guide him to rule his people. Joshua prayed and the sun and the moon stopped moving for a day. Hannah prayed and God gave her Samuel. Elijah prayed and God confirmed his ministry by fire. Jehoshaphat prayed and his stubborn enemies got confused and began to kill themselves.

The people of Nineveh prayed and God gave them mass repentance and national deliverance. Daniel prayed and God closed the mouths of the lions that were starved to eat him up. Esther prayed and the king could not sleep until the decree against God's children was reversed and their enemies avenged. Nehemiah prayed and God gave him a national assignment.

Enoch prayed and God empowered him to walk with him until the day he left this world. Jacob prayed and God changed his name and made him a great prince. Hezekiah prayed and God changed the death verdict that was against him and added fifteen more years to his year. Jabez prayed and God enlarged his coast, removed poverty from him and blessed him mightily. The believers in Peter's day prayed and the prison doors opened and set Peter free. The wife of one of the sons of the prophet prayed and God saved her two sons and she opened an oil company. The daughters of Zelophehad asked Moses a great question. Your father has a name that must not be done away with from among his family. Are you saying that because you are not a man but a woman, your father's possession should be done away with? The daughters of Zelophehad challenged Moses and forced him to release their father's inheritance.

'Why should the name of our father be done away from among his family, because he hath no son? Give unto us therefore a possession among the brethren of our father' (<u>Numbers 27:4</u>).

'And Moses brought their cause before the LORD. And the LORD spake unto Moses, saying, The daughters of Zelophehad speak right: thou shalt surely give them a possession of an inheritance among their father's brethren; and thou shalt cause the inheritance of their father to pass unto them. And thou shalt speak unto the children of Israel, saying, If a man die, and have no son, then ye shall cause his inheritance to pass unto his daughter. And if he have no daughter, then ye shall give his inheritance unto his brethren. And if he have no brethren, then ye shall give his inheritance unto his father's brethren. And if his father have no brethren, then ye shall give his inheritance unto his kinsman that is next to him of his family, and he shall possess it: and it shall be unto the children of Israel a statute of judgment, as the LORD commanded Moses' (<u>Number 27:5-11</u>).

God said that the daughters of Zelophehad were right. Esther went on hunger strike, a suicide prayer mission to save herself and her people. Her prayers gave the king a sleepless night and forced him to request for Esther's presence. Esther's prayers opened the king's mouth to talk to the favor of Esther.

Esther's prayers brought the downfall of her arc enemy and the enemy of God's people called Haman. Her prayers revoked the decree and brought victory to God's children. Her prayers wiped away all tears from God's people, gave them rest, feasts and promoted Mordecai.

It is an insult to God for his own children to remain at the mercies of devil and his agents. The earth, the fullness thereof and people therein belong to God by creation. Many Christians do not know their rights and as a result, they underestimate themselves, undervalue themselves and allow the devil who is the usurper to subtly deceive them to believe his lies concerning who owns all things. Esther, like many believers, originally believed that she could not do anything.

> 'Again Esther spake unto Hatach, and gave him commandment unto Mordecai; All the king's servants, and the people of the king's provinces, do know, that whosoever, whether man or woman, shall come unto the king into the inner court, who is not called, there is one law of his to put him to death, except such to whom the king shall hold out the golden sceptre, that he may live: but I have not been called to come in unto the king these thirty days' (Esther 4:10-11).

It is not God's will for any believer to live a defeated life. It is an insult to accept poverty, sickness or any kind of problem. God himself called us his sons, members of the body of Christ, new creature, beloved of God, brothers to Jesus, temple of God, kings, heirs of God, ambassadors for Christ, peculiar treasure, eagles, and shepherd of the great shepherd

(*See* John 1:12, Matthew 16:18, 2 Corinthians 6:17, John 15:19, Matthew 12:49-50, Ephesians 2:22, Ecclesiastes 8:4, Romans 8:17, 32, 2 Corinthians 5:20, Exodus 19:5, Isaiah 40:31, John 10:11-13).

The agents of devil talk to their master, the devil. When you refuse to pray, you refuse to talk to your God, and God will not do anything until you begin to talk to Him. That is what we call evil silence. I encourage you to pray the prayers here and break yourself loose from evil silence.

> '*Verily I say unto you, Whatsoever ye shall bind on earth shall be bound in heaven: and whatsoever ye shall loose on earth shall be loosed in heaven. Again I say unto you, That if two of you shall agree on earth as touching anything that they shall ask, it shall be done for them of my Father which is in heaven*' (Matthew 18:18-19).

You are not the one who called yourself a new creature, God did. As you repent, confess your sins and forsake them, and stand before Him in prayers as if you have never committed any sin. You must begin to reign as a king upon the earth. King Jesus has the final authority, not the devil, over poverty or any problem in your life. Any circumstance, attitude, curse or utterance contrary to who God said you are can be changed through these prayers.

God is not a failure; therefore, his children must not accept failure. You can use the prayers here to whip the devil, no matter how far or how long he has harassed you in life. When you pray, God will not allow the enemy or demons to defile you, His temple. No strange fire can last in the life of true children of God, who know and believe what God says about them. We belong to God by creation and by redemption and he watches over us to preserve us. If you refuse to acknowledge your sins, confess, repent and forsake them, you rob God of what rightly belong to Him. So, repent before you go into these prayers.

POWERS OF UNOPPOSED ENEMIES

Our generation is filled with realities of lots of impossibilities, un-confronted enemies, negative medical reports, and age long problems, undistracted voices of the enemy and fears of loss or deaths.

> 'And he stood and cried unto the armies of Israel, and said unto them, Why are ye come out to set your battle in array? Am not I a Philistine, and ye servants to Saul? Choose you a man for you, and let him come down to me. If he be able to fight with me, and to kill me, then will we be your servants: but if I prevail against him, and kill him, then shall ye be our servants, and serve us. And the Philistine said, I defy the armies of Israel this day; give me a man, that we may fight together. When Saul and all Israel heard those words of the Philistine, they were dismayed, and greatly afraid. And the Philistine drew near morning and evening, and presented himself forty days. And all the men of Israel, when they saw the man, fled from him, and were sore afraid. And Saul said to David, Thou art not able to go against this Philistine to fight with him: for thou art but a youth, and he a man of war from his youth' (1 Samuel 17:8-11, 16, 24, 33).

Many people see how big their problems are but fail to see how big God is. Goliath stood and cried against the trained armies of Israel. They were not civilians. For forty days, he defied the armies of Israel and made them dismayed and greatly afraid. He drew near and near every morning into the camp of God's children for forty days and made them ran away and become sore afraid of his words.

Many believers, true children of God, cannot get married, bear children, and prosper in everything they do in life. There are no jobs, good accommodation or good salaries to live well. Barrenness, miscarriage, poverty and all manner of problems remain with them to blaspheme God's name.

> *'In those days was Hezekiah sick unto death. And Isaiah the prophet the son of Amoz came unto him, and said unto him, Thus saith the LORD, Set thine house in order: for thou shalt die, and not live'* (Isaiah 38:1).

> *'Then there was a famine in the days of David three years, year after year; and David inquired of the LORD. And the LORD answered, It is for Saul, and for his bloody house, because he slew the Gibeonites'* (2 Samuel 21:1).

When you allow sicknesses, diseases, negative prophecies and visions, they will make you afraid and possibly take you to grave. The battle line is drawn inside the church of Christ. Many are already dismayed and sorely afraid. If you do not rise up and confront your problems, they will never leave on their own.

Hezekiah faced the wall, backed and shun other activates and the negative voice of human being who were compelling him to accept the verdict of death. David decided to face God and he enquired to know why famine and poverty refused to leave his people. He confronted and conquered Goliath to deliver a whole nation.

'And the Philistine said to David, Come to me, and I will give thy flesh unto the fowls of the air, and to the beasts of the field. Then said David to the Philistine, Thou comest to me with a sword, and with a spear, and with a shield: but I come to thee in the name of the LORD of hosts, the God of the armies of Israel, whom thou hast defied. This day will the LORD deliver thee into mine hand; and I will smite thee, and take thine head from thee; and I will give the carcasses of the host of the Philistines this day unto the fowls of the air, and to the wild beasts of the earth; that all the earth may know that there is a God in Israel. And all this assembly shall know that the LORD saveth not with sword and spear: for the battle is the LORD's, and he will give you into our hands. And it came to pass, when the Philistine arose, and came and drew nigh to meet David that David hasted, and ran toward the army to meet the Philistine. And David put his hand in his bag, and took thence a stone, and slang it, and smote the Philistine in his forehead that the stone sunk into his forehead; and he fell upon his face to the earth. So David prevailed over the Philistine with a sling and with a stone, and smote the Philistine, and slew him; but there was no sword in the hand of David' (<u>1 Samuel 17:44-50</u>).

If you do not start fighting, or praying more than you used to pray, you may die in your bondage. Our God is bigger than any problem in life and you need to go to him in prayer. This book can guide and assist you to pray the right prayers. It is wrong to jump into prayer all the time. You need to plan for it, make provision for prayer.

Chapter 5

WARFARE SECTION

1 DAY PRAYER TO KEEP YOUR MARRIAGE OUT OF TROUBLES

1. Every trouble in my marriage, be troubled, in the name of Jesus.

2. Anything standing against my marriage, die now, in the name of Jesus.

3. Let the power of God waste all problems in my marriage, in the name of Jesus.

4. Father Lord, I invite You fully into my marriage, in the name of Jesus.

5. Every seed of marital failures planted against my life, die, in the name of Jesus.

6. Any evil veil covering the face of my partner, burn to ashes, in the name of Jesus.

7. Let the strange love pulling my partner away from me die, in the name of Jesus.

8. I disconnect any evil relationship attacking my marriage, in the name of Jesus.

9. Any evil personality militating against my marriage, die, in the name of Jesus.

10. Any curse placed upon my marriage, expire by force, in the name of Jesus.

11. Any arrow of shame fired against my marriage, backfire, in the name of Jesus.

12. Any evil shadow in my marriage, disappear forever, in the name of Jesus.

13. Any witch or wizard that has vowed to waste my marriage, fail, in the name of Jesus.

14. Any Goliath anointed to kill my marriage, die by force, in the name of Jesus.

15. Every stronghold built against my marriage, collapse, in the name of Jesus.

16. Every serpent in the garden of my marriage, die, in the name of Jesus.

17. Every satanic poison in my marriage, dry up, in the name of Jesus.

18. Let the activities of the wicked in my marriage be terminated, in the name of Jesus.

19. Every problem in my marriage, I cut you off forever, in the name of Jesus.

20. O Lord, deliver my marriage from all manner of troubles, in the name of Jesus.

3 DAYS PRAYER TO KEEP YOUR MARRIAGE OUT OF TROUBLES

1. Any serpent in the garden of my marriage, stretch yourself and die, in the name of Jesus.

2. Any evil voice that is speaking against my marriage, be silenced forever, in the name of Jesus.

3. Let that power assigned to contradict God in my home be disgraced, in the name of Jesus.

4. Father Lord, design and commission my marriage, in the name of Jesus.

5. Any evil personality speaking to my life partner, I cut off your head, in the name of Jesus.

6. Any stranger that has entered into my home, walk out by force, in the name of Jesus.

7. Let every door the enemy has opened in my home be closed forever, in the name of Jesus.

8. Any evil voice attacking God's Word in my marriage, be silenced by force, in the name of Jesus.

9. Let every contrary command opposing God's command in my life be rejected, in the name of Jesus.

10. O Lord, uphold Your place in my home forever, in the name of Jesus.

11. Any evil personality that wants to take God's place in my home, die, in the name of Jesus.

12. Whoever has vowed to introduce sin into my family must be disgraced, in the name of Jesus.

13. I command the author of sin in my home to die with his sin, in the name of Jesus.

14. Every agent of wrong choice in my home, die without mercy, in the name of Jesus.

15. Any evil step taken already in my home, be reversed, in the name of Jesus.

16. Any man or woman that is attacking the peace of this marriage, be frustrated, in the name of Jesus.

17. O Lord, let nobody in my family admit the devil and his agent, in the name of Jesus.

18. Any invitation given to the devil in my marriage, I withdraw you, in the name of Jesus.

19. I close every ears in my family from listening to the lies of the enemy, in the name of Jesus.

20. Any messenger of devil in my marriage, carry your message back, in the name of Jesus.

21. Owners of evil loads in my family, carry your load, in the name of Jesus.

1. Any evil word spoken against my marriage, expire by force, in the name of Jesus.

2. Every word opposed to the truth in my family, be rejected immediately, in the name of Jesus.

3. Any darkness in any part of my family, disappear by force, in the name of Jesus.

4. Any stubborn agent of darkness in my family, be exposed and disgraced, in the name of Jesus.

5. Any evil leg that has walked into my family, walk out by force, in the name of Jesus.

6. Let the judgment fire of God fall upon every enemy of my marriage, in the name of Jesus.

7. Any evil eye monitoring my family, be blinded, in the name of Jesus.

8. Any discussion anywhere against my marriage, be converted to foolishness, in the name of Jesus.

9. Let the lies of the devil be frustrated in my family, in the name of Jesus.

10. O Lord, deliver everyone in my family from looking at what You have forbidden, in the name of Jesus.

11. Any evil personality that has vowed to bring sin into my family, fail woefully, in the name of Jesus.

12. O Lord, arise and cleanse my home with Your cleansing power, in the name of Jesus.

13. Father Lord, deliver every member of my family from eating forbidden fruits, in the name of Jesus.

14. Blood of Jesus, purge my home with Your blood, in the name of Jesus.

15. Let the sins of everyone in my family receive pardon today, in the name of Jesus.

16. Heavenly father, come back to my family with Your glory, in the name of Jesus.

17. Any evil plantation in my home, be uprooted, in the name of Jesus.

18. Let every evil the devil has introduced in my home be rejected, in the name of Jesus.

19. Holy Ghost fire, enter into every heart in my family and cleanse it, in the name of Jesus.

20. Any witchcraft animal living in my family, be exposed unto death, in the name of Jesus.

21. Lord Jesus, empower everyone in my family to hate sin, in the name of Jesus.

22. Every enemy of God's Word in my home, die, in the name of Jesus.

23. Let the Word of the Lord reign and rule in my home, in the name of Jesus.

1. Any corrupt person in my family, be exposed and be disgraced, in the name of Jesus.

2. I refuse to bring temptation to any member of my own family, in the name of Jesus.

3. Any spirit of eve in the life of anyone in my family, surrender to God's will, in the name of Jesus.

4. Any evil personality distributing the forbidden fruit to the members of my family, be rejected with your fruit, in the name of Jesus.

5. Let the nature of sin in the hearts of anyone in my family be uprooted, in the name of Jesus.

6. Every demon of guilt and condemnation in my life, be cast out, in the name of Jesus.

7. O Lord, arise and deliver everyone in my family from wicked serpents, in the name of Jesus.

8. Lord Jesus, walk into my family and take over its leadership, in the name of Jesus.

9. O Lord, help me to reverse Your judgment against my family because of sin, in the name of Jesus.

10. Any curse that Satan brought into my family, expire, in the name of Jesus.

11. O Lord, return my family to its original state as of the old, in the name of Jesus.

12. Let the presence of God come back into my family, in the name of Jesus.

13. Any area of my family life that is captured by the devil, be delivered, in the name of Jesus.

14. Father Lord, empower my family to come together to fulfill the purpose of marriage, in the name of Jesus.

15. Let the angel of my marriage bring every good thing that was lost, in the name of Jesus.

16. Every sinful stain, spot and blemish in my family, be cleansed by the blood of Jesus, in the name of Jesus.

17. Let the troubles in my family come to an end today, in the name of Jesus.

18. Every strange personality in my family, I force you out by fire, in the name of Jesus.

19. Father Lord, bring back Your love in my marriage by fire, in the name of Jesus.

20. Let the mercy of God begin to enter into my family by God's grace, in the name of Jesus.

21. Let the speaking blood of Christ speak peace and unity back into my home, in the name of Jesus.

22. Every demonic enemy of my marriage, be beheaded, in the name of Jesus.

23. Let all the departed glory of my marriage come back by fire, in the name of Jesus.

21. O Lord, arise and end every war going on against my marriage, in the name of Jesus.

5 DAYS PRAYER TO KEEP YOUR MARRIAGE OUT OF TROUBLES

1. Let the perfect life of Christ and his wonderful teachings rule in my home, in the name of Jesus.

2. Father Lord, release Your divine provision into my family today, in the name of Jesus.

3. Let the anointing blood of Christ flow into my family for immediate deliverance, in the name of Jesus.

4. Blood of Jesus, flow into my marriage foundation and liberate my home, in the name of Jesus.

5. I command my marriage to receive full redemption from the death of Jesus, in the name of Jesus.

6. Every problem in my family, be wasted by the death of Jesus, in the name of Jesus.

7. Blood of Jesus, bring full salvation into my family today, in the name of Jesus.

8. Let the victorious death of Christ enter into my marriage today for deliverance, in the name of Jesus.

9. Blood of Jesus, enter into my home and speak death to all my troubles, in the name of Jesus.

10. Let every blessing my marriage has lost begin to come back double, in the name of Jesus.

11. Every good thing that the devil and sin have stolen from my marriage, receive life now, in the name of Jesus.

12. Lord Jesus, please come back fully into my marriage, in the name of Jesus.

13. Any outstanding restitution to be done in my marriage, O Lord, help me to do it, in the name of Jesus.

14. Blood of Jesus, blot out every sin in my marriage, in the name of Jesus.

15. Let there be pardon and remission of sins in my home, in the name of Jesus.

16. I command the reconciling power of God to manifest in my family, in the name of Jesus.

17. Father Lord, send Your heavenly joy and peace into my family, in the name of Jesus.

18. Every corruption in my family, be destroyed by the grace of God, in the name of Jesus.

19. Father Lord, command Your divine security to manifest in my marriage, in the name of Jesus.

20. Let divine obedience begin to rule and reign in my family, in the name of Jesus.

21. Father Lord, make everyone in my family a new creature in Christ Jesus, in the name of Jesus.

22. Let the defeated eagle of my marriage begin to fly again, in the name of Jesus.

23. Holy Ghost fire, burn to ashes every problem in my marriage, in the name of Jesus.

1. Father Lord, restore my lost marriage's godly altar, in the name of Jesus.

2. Let all the good desires of my marriage begin to manifest by fire, in the name of Jesus.

3. Every tears of prayers offered for my marriage, receive answers, in the name of Jesus.

4. O Lord, let my cry for blessings in my marriage receive divine attention, in the name of Jesus.

5. Every supplication ever made for my marriage, receive answer, in the name of Jesus.

6. Every instinct, appeal and calling ever directed to God in prayer for my marriage, receive answers now, in the name of Jesus.

7. Let the groaning, weeping and agonies of prayer for my marriage receive immediate answers, in the name of Jesus.

8. Any spirit attacking the headship in this marriage, die, in the name of Jesus.

9. Any power that has disorganized God's ordained order in this marriage, die, in the name of Jesus.

10. O Lord, restore Your divine ordained order in this marriage, in the name of Jesus.

11. Let the man of the house take over his position as the head, in the name of Jesus.

12. O Lord, empower the husband to meet up with his responsibilities, in the name of Jesus.

13. Let the wife's loving submission to the husband be upheld, in the name of Jesus.

14. I command the wife to recognize and joyfully accept God's ordained order, in the name of Jesus.

15. Let no one ever question the headship of the man of the house, in the name of Jesus.

16. Let everyone in the home be given his or her merits, in the name of Jesus.

17. Let every plan of God for this home begin to manifest by fire, in the name of Jesus.

18. Power to submit as unto the Lord by the woman, manifest, in the name of Jesus.

19. Every evil presence in this marriage, be destroyed by fire, in the name of Jesus.

20. Any evil personality sitting on the throne of this marriage, be unseated, in the name of Jesus.

21. Blood of Jesus, flow into the root of this marriage for deliverance, in the name of Jesus.

22. O Lord, arise and take Your rightful place in this marriage, in the name of Jesus.

23. Every enemy of this marriage, be exposed and disgraced, in the name of Jesus.

24. Holy Ghost fire, burn to ashes every problem in this marriage, in the name of Jesus.

Day 3

1. Let the presence of old selves in this marriage disappear, in the name of Jesus.

2. Father Lord, empower everyone in this family to have encounter with Christ, in the name of Jesus.

3. Let the grace of God that will make every member of this family a new creature come now, in the name of Jesus.

4. Let the anointing of true repentance fall upon everyone in this family, in the name of Jesus.

5. I command every old thing in the life of everyone in this family to die, in the name of Jesus.

6. O Lord, empower us in this family to have a new relationship with You, in the name of Jesus.

7. Let everyone's life in this family be delivered from the deeds of the old self, in the name of Jesus.

8. I command the activities of the devil in this home to end, in the name of Jesus.

9. Every root of carnality in this family, be uprooted, in the name of Jesus.

10. Let the spirit of lying in this family be cast out forever, in the name of Jesus.

11. Every enemy of truth in this family, expire and be disgraced, in the name of Jesus.

12. Blood of Jesus, empower everyone in this family to embrace truth, in the name of Jesus.

13. Any spirit of stealing, you are wicked, come out and die, in the name of Jesus.

14. Every serpent in the tongue of anyone in this family, die, in the name of Jesus.

15. Any power that speaks evil in this family, I cast you out, in the name of Jesus.

16. Let the spirit of bitterness and wrath in this family be cast out, in the name of Jesus.

17. I bind and cast out the spirit of anger and clamor in this family, in the name of Jesus.

18. Blood of Jesus, destroy the spirit of malice in this family, in the name of Jesus.

19. Any power in this family that grieves the spirit of God, be destroyed, in the name of Jesus.

20. Every work of flesh in this home, die, in the name of Jesus.

21. Angels of the living God, take over this family from now, in the name of Jesus.

22. Holy Ghost fire, burn to ashes every enemy of this family, in the name of Jesus.

1. O Lord, empower everyone in this family to put away the deeds of the old man and self, in the name of Jesus.

2. Let the manifestation of the old man and self in this family die by fire, in the name of Jesus.

3. Let my family move from the camp of the old man to the camp of new man, in the name of Jesus.

4. Any place given to the devil in my family, be recovered by force, in the name of Jesus.

5. O Lord, deliver my home from the practice of sentiments, in the name of Jesus.

6. Let everyone in this home remain loving without compromise, in the name of Jesus.

7. Lord, help us in this family to be soft to each other, yet firm to please You , in the name of Jesus.

8. Father Lord, help us to love even sinner but hate their sins with perfect hatred, in the name of Jesus.

9. Blood of Jesus, renew the mind of everyone in this family today, in the name of Jesus.

10. O Lord, help us to enjoy the benefits of a new creature in this family, in the name of Jesus.

11. Father Lord, empower everyone in this family to take Your command seriously, in the name of Jesus.

12. I bind and cast out any power that has vowed to displace truth in this family, in the name of Jesus.

13. O Lord, help us to obey the Word of God as it is written, in the name of Jesus.

14. Let everyone in this family possess true holiness to the end, in the name of Jesus.

15. Let the throne of the devil in this home be roasted by fire, in the name of Jesus.

16. I command every evil presence in this family to disappear by force, in the name of Jesus.

17. O Lord, help everyone in this family to work and labor to Your glory, in the name of Jesus.

18. Let every speech in this family be well spoken and seasoned, in the name of Jesus.

19. Father Lord, help us to learn and practice how to relate with one another in this family, in the name of Jesus.

20. I command the spirit of fighting and quarrelling to depart from this family, in the name of Jesus.

21. Power to forgive and forget, possess every member of this family, in the name of Jesus.

22. O Lord, arise and take over the lives of everyone in this family, in the name of Jesus.

23. Let divine presence dominate every place in this family, in the name of Jesus.

Day 5

1. Let everyone in this family receive dominion over sin, Satan and sickness, in the name of Jesus.

2. I command every work of the flesh in this home to die, in the name of Jesus.

3. Let the stripes of Christ destroy every sickness in this family, in the name of Jesus.

4. Any power contesting with the Spirit of Christ in this family, die, in the name of Jesus.

5. O Lord, give us spiritual victory in this family, in the name of Jesus.

6. Let competition of holy living increase in the life of every member of this family, in the name of Jesus.

7. Let Jesus Christ be enthroned in the life of everyone in this family, in the name of Jesus.

8. I command the throne of trouble in this family to collapse, in the name of Jesus.

9. I command every self in this family to be crucified, in the name of Jesus.

10. Every presence of Adamic depravity in this family, be removed by force, in the name of Jesus.

11. Let holiness and complete victory be a daily experience in this family, in the name of Jesus.

12. Let every member of this family begin to please God at all cost, in the name of Jesus.

13. O Lord help every member of this family to conform totally to the image of Christ, in the name of Jesus.

14. Every reproach, shame and disgrace in this family, die by force, in the name of Jesus.

15. Let Jesus Christ's life be our pattern in this family forever, in the name of Jesus.

16. Father Lord, impart in us the true love of Christ in this family, in the name of Jesus.

17. Let the measurement of our love be practical as Jesus' love, in the name of Jesus.

18. Let our standards of love in this family be sacrificial like that of Jesus, in the name of Jesus.

19. Let lusts, fornication and uncleanness never be at any time mentioned in this family, in the name of Jesus.

20. I command the spirit of covetousness and filthiness to depart from this family, in the name of Jesus.

21. Father Lord, deliver us from foolish talking, jesting and works of iniquity, in the name of Jesus.

22. O Lord, help us to walk in light forever in this family, in the name of Jesus.

7 DAYS PRAYER TO KEEP YOUR MARRIAGE OUT OF TROUBLE

1. Let the presence of God be restored double in this family, in the name of Jesus.

2. O Lord, empower everyone in my family to do all things that pleases You, in the name of Jesus.

3. Let the love that suffers long, and is kind enter into my family and rule, in the name of Jesus.

4. Father Lord, release into my family the love that has no envy and pride, in the name of Jesus.

5. I command every indignity, opposition and gossips in my family to clear away now, in the name of Jesus.

6. O Lord, help me to overcome anger in my life and embrace divine love in my family, in the name of Jesus.

7. Any spirit of retaliation in my home, I cast you out forever, in the name of Jesus.

8.   O Lord, help me to react with kindness in my home in every situation, in the name of Jesus.

9.   Let every pregnancy of anger, wrath, malice, hatred, bitterness and retaliation be aborted in my home forever, in the name of Jesus.

10. Let the spirit of deeply rooted envy, jealous, pride, self-exaltation and self-praise in my home be unseated by force, in the name of Jesus.

11. Any spirit of bragging and boasting in my family, I cast you out forever, in the name of Jesus.

12. O Lord, give me the humility that can never entertain quarrel or argument, in the name of Jesus.

13. Any spirit of pride in my home, leave at once, in the name of Jesus.

14. Father Lord, give me a love that is considerate towards others, in the name of Jesus.

15. Let love that is disciplined in behavior possess me by fire, in the name of Jesus.

16. I refuse to act without considering God's Word or the happiness of others, in the name of Jesus.

17. O Lord, deliver me from rudeness and bad character, in the name of Jesus.

18. Every spirit of rudeness or improper behavior in my life, die by force, in the name of Jesus.

19. Any power that makes me to act disorderly, I cast you out of my home, in the name of Jesus.

20. Let the demon of self-centeredness depart forever from my home, in the name of Jesus.

21. Father Lord, direct every conversation and actions in my home, in the name of Jesus.

22. Blood of Jesus, flow into the foundation of my home and restore all the good things we have lost, in the name of Jesus.

1. O Lord, empower us to do Your will in our home as it is done in heaven, in the name of Jesus.

2. O Lord, sanctify everyone in my home and give us inner victory and freedom, in the name of Jesus.

3. Father Lord, give us power of unity and perfect love in my family, in the name of Jesus.

4. Let the power of the Holy Ghost keep every motive in my family pure, in the name of Jesus.

5. Let the love for God and His Word and for one another reign and rule in this home, in the name of Jesus.

6. Let the love of God in the hearts of everyone in this family be expressed outwardly, in the name of Jesus.

7. Let the profession of love in my family manifest in deeds of kindness to one another, in the name of Jesus.

8. I command everyone in my family to take the office of a servant, in the name of Jesus.

9. Let the simplicity and the sincerity of Christ manifest in my marriage, in the name of Jesus.

10. Every victory that has eluded my marriage, be recovered double, in the name of Jesus.

11. O Lord, deliver my marriage from the control of spiritual enemies, in the name of Jesus.

12. Any power that wants my family to backslide, be wasted, in the name of Jesus.

13. Let the power of love that will make me and my partner to walk together, possess us, in the name of Jesus.

14. Power to live in peace, possess us, in the name of Jesus.

15. Power to rejoice together, possess us, in the name of Jesus.

16. Power to comfort one another, possess us, in the name of Jesus.

17. Power to exhort one another, possess us, in the name of Jesus.

18. Power to admonish one another, possess us, in the name of Jesus.

19. Power to forebear one another, possess us, in the name of Jesus.

20. Power to submit to one another, possess us, in the name of Jesus.

21. Power to prefer one another, possess us, in the name of Jesus.

22. Power to bear each other's burden, possess us, in the name of Jesus.

23. Power to take care of one another, possess us, in the name of Jesus.

24. Power to consider each another, possess us, in the name of Jesus.

25. Power to edify one another, possess us, in the name of Jesus.

26. Power to minister to each other's need, possess us, in the name of Jesus.

27. Power to forgive one another, possess us, in the name of Jesus.

28. Power to greet each other, possess us, in the name of Jesus.

29. Power to teach one another, possess us, in the name of Jesus.

30. Power to pray for each other, possess us, in the name of Jesus.

31. O Lord, bring back divine confidence we once had for each other, in the name of Jesus.

32. Let my partner and I agree in goals, aspiration and lifestyle, in the name of Jesus.

33. O Lord, help me and my partner to trust each other, in the name of Jesus.

34. O Lord, help us to be faithful to our vows to the end, in the name of Jesus.

35. I receive power to separate myself from sin and submit to God and remain prayerful, in the name of Jesus.

36. O Lord, help us to avoid pitfalls on our way to victory, in the name of Jesus.

37. O Lord, help me and my partner to have enough time to fellowship together, in the name of Jesus.

38. Every physical hindrance on our way in this marriage journey, be removed, in the name of Jesus.

39. Every enemy of my marriage, be exposed and disgraced, in the name of Jesus.

1. Every spirit against holiness in my home, die, in the name of Jesus.

2. Any arrow of poverty fired at my home to scatter it, backfire, in the name of Jesus.

3. Any evil mark fashioned to destroy my marriage, catch fire, in the name of Jesus.

4. O Lord, shower Your blessings into my marriage to save my home, in the name of Jesus.

5. Every enemy of peace in my home, be disgraced by force, in the name of Jesus.

6. Father Lord, plant Your true hope and joy in my family, in the name of Jesus.

7. Blood of Jesus, destroy every seed of grief planted against my marriage, in the name of Jesus.

8. O Lord, start a new thing in my family to save my marriage, in the name of Jesus.

9. Any evil existing in my marriage, be uprooted by fire of God, in the name of Jesus.

10. Any evil mouth opened against my marriage, close in shame, in the name of Jesus.

11. O Lord, bring divine laughter to my marriage again, in the name of Jesus.

12. O Lord, plant Your fruit of joy and peace in my marriage, in the name of Jesus.

13. Let divine solutions begin to manifest in my family by force, in the name of Jesus.

14. O Lord, arise and perfect Your work in my marriage, in the name of Jesus.

15. Let my marriage be built upon the solid rock of God, in the name of Jesus.

16. Any witch or wizard attacking my family finance, be disgraced, in the name of Jesus.

17. O Lord, empower me to prevail over every enemy of my marriage, in the name of Jesus.

18. I command supernatural blessings to come upon my marriage, in the name of Jesus.

19. My marriage will not die as result of problems against it, in the name of Jesus.

20. I command the eagle of my marriage to arise and fly high, in the name of Jesus.

21. Blood of Jesus, speak progression into my marriage by fire, in the name of Jesus.

Day 4

1. Any satanic altar against my marriage, catch fire and scatter, in the name of Jesus.

2. I command my marriage, to come out from every demonic coffin, in the name of Jesus.

3. Every witchcraft terror in my marriage, disappear, in the name of Jesus.

4. Any evil that has invaded my marriage, disappear by force, in the name of Jesus.

5. Every departed glory of my marriage, come back by force, in the name of Jesus.

6. Let the beauty of my marriage return double, in the name of Jesus.

7. O Lord, empower me to see the end of every problem in my marriage, in the name of Jesus.

8. Whosoever must be disgraced for my marriage to prosper, be disgraced, in the name of Jesus.

9. Any satanic preference in my marriage, disappear forever, in the name of Jesus.

10. Let the Lord's blessing stolen by the enemy be restored in my marriage, in the name of Jesus.

11. Every evil speech made against my marriage, die by force, in the name of Jesus.

12. Any graveyard that has buried my marriage, release it now, in the name of Jesus.

13. Let the abundant life of Christ enter into my dead marriage now, in the name of Jesus.

14. I command my marriage to move from the valley to the mountaintop, in the name of Jesus.

15. O Lord, cloth my marriage with your divine beauty, in the name of Jesus.

16. Every seed of pride and jealousy in my marriage, die, in the name of Jesus.

17. Any problem that has captured my marriage, disappear by force, in the name of Jesus.

18. Any strange fire burning in my marriage, quench, in the name of Jesus.

19. Any yoke of marital breakup in my marriage, break to pieces, in the name of Jesus.

20. Let every evil movement against my marriage be arrested, in the name of Jesus.

21. Blood of Jesus, deliver my marriage from marriage destroyers, in the name of Jesus.

1. Let every enemy of my marriage become restless until they repent and surrender, in the name of Jesus.

2. Every war going on against my marriage, end to my favor, in the name of Jesus.

3. I command every yoke of failure in my marriage to break, in the name of Jesus.

4. Every arrow of disgrace fired against my marriage, backfire, in the name of Jesus.

5. Every stubborn enemy of my marriage, be electrocuted by fire, in the name of Jesus.

6. I recover every virtue that was stolen from my marriage, in the name of Jesus.

7. Every Red Sea assigned to carry my marriage away, dry up, in the name of Jesus.

8. Let the roots of my marital problems be consumed by fire, in the name of Jesus.

9. Every satanic success against my marriage, be converted to failure, in the name of Jesus.

10. Any evil attack going on against my marriage, be terminated, in the name of Jesus.

11. Let the spirit of faultfinding working against my marriage die, in the name of Jesus.

12. Any power that has vowed to destroy my marriage and me, be destroyed, in the name of Jesus.

13. O Lord, bring Your breakthrough into my marriage, in the name of Jesus.

14. Every blessing that my marriage has lost, be recovered double, in the name of Jesus.

15. O Lord, arise and enlarge the coast of my marriage, in the name of Jesus.

16. Every dream of failure against my marriage, be aborted, in the name of Jesus.

17. Father Lord, arise and promote my marriage by fire, in the name of Jesus.

18. Let divine program for my marriage begin to manifest, in the name of Jesus.

19. Every satanic padlock that is locking my marriage in sorrow, break, in the name of Jesus.

20. Let the power of the devil against my marriage be destroyed, in the name of Jesus.

1. O Lord, arise and fulfill Your divine purpose over my marriage, in the name of Jesus.

2. Let the fruits of the Holy Spirit manifest in my marriage by fire, in the name of Jesus.

3. Every seed of rigidity attacking my marriage, die by fire, in the name of Jesus.

4. Any evil mind conspiring against my marriage, be confused, in the name of Jesus.

5. Any evil brain thinking against my marriage, scatter by fire, in the name of Jesus.

6. Let every part of my marriage's heaven that is closed open, in the name of Jesus.

7. Every good thing the devil has sized from my marriage, be released now, in the name of Jesus.

8. Any Jezebel or Delilah attacking my marriage, die, in the name of Jesus.

9. Any contrary wind blowing against my marriage, cease, in the name of Jesus.

10. Any evil vow troubling my marriage, be revoked by force, in the name of Jesus.

11. Let every darkness covering the light of my marriage disappear, in the name of Jesus.

12. Let the host of hell fire gathering against my marriage scatter, in the name of Jesus.

13. I command my marriage to cooperate with God for heavenly support, in the name of Jesus.

14. Let every enemy of my marriage experience great downfall, in the name of Jesus.

15. Every wicked gang-up against my marriage, be broken, in the name of Jesus.

16. Any witch or wizard that has vowed to scatter my marriage, be disgraced, in the name of Jesus.

17. Any evil plan against my marriage, backfire by force, in the name of Jesus.

18. Father Lord, disgrace and disappoint enemies of my marriage, in the name of Jesus.

19. Every evil step that was taken against my marriage, I put you to shame, in the name of Jesus.

20. Any bitterness existing in my marriage, be converted to joy and peace, in the name of Jesus.

21. Father Lord, deliver my marriage from collapse, in the name of Jesus.

1. Let divine love take over my marriage, in the name of Jesus.

2. Every spirit of fear and death in my marriage, disappear by force, in the name of Jesus.

3. Let every witchcraft conspiracy against my marriage fail woefully, in the name of Jesus.

4. Let divine goodness for my marriage begin to manifest from now, in the name of Jesus.

5. Every evil tongue raised against my marriage, be silenced, in the name of Jesus.

6. Every seed of deceit planted against my marriage, die, in the name of Jesus.

7. Let all evil devices of the enemy against my marriage backfire, in the name of Jesus.

8. Let the craftiness of the water spirit against my marriage be wasted, in the name of Jesus.

9. Every demonic wisdom against my marriage, be destroyed, in the name of Jesus.

10. Every evil sacrifice offered against my marriage, expire, in the name of Jesus.

11. Every spirit of destruction working against my marriage, be destroyed, in the name of Jesus.

12. Holy Ghost fire, burn to ashes every problem in my marriage, in the name of Jesus.

13. Let all that is troubling of my marriage be troubled unto death, in the name of Jesus.

14. Let my marriage become too hot for the devil to operate in, in the name of Jesus.

15. Every evil force against my marriage, stumble and fall forever, in the name of Jesus.

16. Every curse working against my marriage, expire forever, in the name of Jesus.

17. Let the spirit of Goliath against my marriage die by fire, in the name of Jesus.

18. Any power prolonging my marital success, be executed by force, in the name of Jesus.

19. Any problem from hell in my marriage, return back in defeat, in the name of Jesus.

20. O Lord, reveal to me what to do to deliver my marriage from trouble, in the name of Jesus.

21. You, my marriage, rise and shine, in the name of Jesus.

14 DAYS PRAYER TO KEEP YOUR MARRIAGE OUT OF TROUBLES

1. Any evil personality that is causing havoc in my marriage, be disgraced, in the name of Jesus.

2. Any strange fire burning in my marriage, I put you off, in the name of Jesus.

3. Any power promoting faultfinding and unforgiving spirit in my marriage, die, in the name of Jesus.

4. Blood of Jesus, help me to fulfill the purpose of God for my marriage, in the name of Jesus.

5. Every evil cloud surrounding my marriage, be cleared away, in the name of Jesus.

6. Any evil wind blowing against my marriage, be diverted, in the name of Jesus.

7. Let God's goodness that has eluded my marriage begin to come back, in the name of Jesus.

8. Any evil covenant troubling my marriage, break, in the name of Jesus.

9. I command arrested star of my marriage to appear, in the name of Jesus.

10. Any witchcraft pillar mounted against my marriage, be uprooted, in the name of Jesus.

11. Father Lord, command victory and liberty into my marriage, in the name of Jesus.

12. Every Goliath fighting against my marriage, I cut off your head, in the name of Jesus.

13. Let the reign of the flesh in my marriage be terminated, in the name of Jesus.

14. Every evil judgment against my marriage, be converted to victory, in the name of Jesus.

15. Father Lord, send Your angel in charge of my marriage back to my home, in the name of Jesus.

16. Any unprofitable quarrel going on in my home, die, in the name of Jesus.

17. Let the fire of God chase away every demonic fire in my home, in the name of Jesus.

18. O Lord arise, and deliver my marriage from collapsing, in the name of Jesus.

19.   Any evil gathering against my marriage, scatter in shame, in the name of Jesus.

20.   Every burden upon my marriage, be lifted by force, in the name of Jesus.

21.   Blood of Jesus, speak destruction unto every problem in my marriage, in the name of Jesus.

1. Any power that has vowed to bring separation into my marriage, die, in the name of Jesus.

2. Every spirit of conflict and hostility in my home, be cast out, in the name of Jesus.

3. Every demon of divorce that is militating against my marriage, be disgraced, in the name of Jesus.

4. Blood of Jesus, bring unity from above into my family, in the name of Jesus.

5. Let demonic darkness in my marriage disappear by force, in the name of Jesus.

6. I command my marriage to be too hot for marriage breakers, in the name of Jesus.

7. Any war going on against my marriage, end to my favor, in the name of Jesus.

8. Let the angel of God torment every enemy of my marriage until they bow, in the name of Jesus.

9. Father Lord, let Your light of peace be directed into my marriage, in the name of Jesus.

10. Let the spirit of worldliness and luxury attacking my family be wasted, in the name of Jesus.

11. Any spiritual burial against my marriage, be resurrected, in the name of Jesus.

12. Let the powers of darkness that have taken over my marriage be frustrated, in the name of Jesus.

13. You the spirit of Beelzebub against my marriage, be destroyed, in the name of Jesus.

14. Any power that wants to control my marriage against God's will, die, in the name of Jesus.

15. Let every evil prison that has locked up my marriage release it now, in the name of Jesus.

16. Any spirit of divorce that has vowed to destroy my marriage, die by fire, in the name of Jesus.

17. Any evil counsel given against my marriage, be rejected, in the name of Jesus.

18. I command every Judas in my marriage to be disgraced, in the name of Jesus.

19. Any false information designed to scatter my marriage, fade away, in the name of Jesus.

20. Let the wicked powers persecuting my marriage be destroyed, in the name of Jesus.

21. Every satanic interest over my marriage, be frustrated, in the name of Jesus.

22. Blood of Jesus, flow into my marriage for deliverance, in the name of Jesus.

1. Any power from the waters waging their head against my marriage, die, in the name of Jesus.

2. I command every witchcraft vinegar in my marriage to be converted to honey, in the name of Jesus.

3. Let any agent of darkness deceiving my partner or myself be disgraced, in the name of Jesus.

4. Any evil chain holding my marriage in bondage, break, in the name of Jesus.

5. Let the love of riches attacking my marriage be cast out, in the name of Jesus.

6. Any evil tradition or custom that has sold my marriage to the devil, die, in the name of Jesus.

7. I break and loose my marriage from the captivity of evil forces, in the name of Jesus.

8. Father Lord, help me and my partner to develop matured life of discipline, in the name of Jesus.

9. I command my temperament and that of my partner to be developed according God's terms, in the name of Jesus.

10. Father Lord, help me to practice self-denial and unselfish lifestyle, in the name of Jesus.

11. Any spirit of laziness in my family attacking my marriage, die, in the name of Jesus.

12. Any spirit of anger and murder in my family, be cast out, in the name of Jesus.

13. O Lord, help me not to plan anything further in my family without You, in the name of Jesus.

14. Any serpent of impatience working against my marriage, be destroyed, in the name of Jesus.

15. Any wickedness that was designed to waste my marriage, be exposed and disgraced, in the name of Jesus.

16. Let the serpent of drunkenness against my marriage be cast out, in the name of Jesus.

17. Let every spirit of lying and conspiracy against my marriage, die, in the name of Jesus.

18. I command every spirit of immorality and suspicion to die, in the name of Jesus.

19. Any enchantment and divination against my marriage, expire, in the name of Jesus.

20. I cast out every spirit of murmur, complaints and discouragement, in the name of Jesus.

21. Any bad influence that is working against my marriage, be terminated, in the name of Jesus.

22. Any evil force blocking my marriage from reaching the Promised Land, scatter, in the name of Jesus.

23. O Lord, arise and command my marriage to move forward, in the name of Jesus.

1. Any accursed thing working against my marriage, I take you away, in the name of Jesus.

2. Any remnant of the devil in my marriage, receive divine judgment, in the name of Jesus.

3. Any evil priest ministering against my marriage, die, in the name of Jesus.

4. Let that evil altar built specifically against my marriage burn to ashes, in the name of Jesus.

5. Any evil in the presence of my marriage, disappear by force, in the name of Jesus.

6. Let all evil forces encamped against my marriage scatter, in the name of Jesus.

7. Any familiar spirit attacking my marriage, be cast out, in the name of Jesus.

8. Any evil accusation designed to scatter my marriage, be exposed, in the name of Jesus.

9. Any disgrace planned against my marriage, be disgraced, in the name of Jesus.

10. I command the arrows of adultery fired against my marriage to backfire, in the name of Jesus.

11. Any evil personality that has stolen the heart of my partner, die, in the name of Jesus.

12. I cast out every spirit of lust for strange women or men in my life, in the name of Jesus.

13. Every yoke of polygamy and polyandry in my family, break, in the name of Jesus.

14. Any false prophesy against my marriage, expire, in the name of Jesus.

15. Every enemy of my marriage in disguise, be exposed and disgraced, in the name of Jesus.

16. I command every sexual demon that has vowed to destroy my marriage to die, in the name of Jesus.

17. Any wall of Jericho blocking my marriage, collapse, in the name of Jesus.

18. Any problem mocking my marriage, fall down and die, in the name of Jesus.

19. Let the fire of God burn every strange woman or man in my marriage, in the name of Jesus.

20. Any witchcraft incense burning for the sake of my marriage, I put you off, in the name of Jesus.

21. Any evil king or queen sitting upon my marriage, be unseated by death, in the name of Jesus.

22. Let my marriage escape the arrows of separation and divorce, in the name of Jesus.

1. Any arrow of fear fired into my marriage, backfire, in the name of Jesus.

2. Blood of Jesus, remove any blood crying against this marriage, in the name of Jesus.

3. Any unnecessary battle going on against my marriage, be terminated, in the name of Jesus.

4. Anything in this marriage rebelling against God, be destroyed, in the name of Jesus.

5. Any evil spirit on assignment against my marriage, die, in the name of Jesus.

6. O Lord, give me a counsel that will restore your presence in this marriage, in the name of Jesus.

7. Any area this marriage has forsaken God, O Lord, forgive us and come back, in the name of Jesus.

8. O Lord, help my family to serve You with a perfect heart, in the name of Jesus.

9. Father Lord, deliver my marriage from satanic mockery, in the name of Jesus.

10. Let the defilements, corruptions and pollutions in this marriage be cleansed, in the name of Jesus.

11. I terminate idolatry in this family by force, in the name of Jesus.

12. Every demon of cheat and defeat in this marriage, die, in the name of Jesus.

13. Every serpent of boasting and hypocrisy in my family, be destroyed, in the name of Jesus.

14. Let my marriage be delivered from spirit of pride and arrogance, in the name of Jesus.

15. Anything in my marriage provoking God to anger, die forever, in the name of Jesus.

16. I command my marriage to embrace God perfectly, in the name of Jesus.

17. Any spirit of rage, fury and violence in my marriage, be destroyed forever, in the name of Jesus.

18. Any power postponing divine deliverance of my marriage, die, in the name of Jesus.

19. Anything that has made my marriage unclean, catch fire, burn to ashes, in the name of Jesus.

20. Any evil plot against my marriage, be discovered and destroyed, in the name of Jesus.

21. Any problem hired to grieve, scorn and torment my marriage, die, in the name of Jesus.

22. You my marriage, receive true deliverance, in the name of Jesus.

1. Any evil chamber in my marriage, catch fire by force, in the name of Jesus.

2. Any treacherous demons tormenting my marriage, die by fire, in the name of Jesus.

3. Father Lord, remove every curse placed upon my marriage, in the name of Jesus.

4. Any power that is promoting evil in my marriage, be destroyed, in the name of Jesus.

5. Let the oppressors of my marriage cease and be oppressed, in the name of Jesus.

6. Any power pursuing my marriage into error, fall down and die, in the name of Jesus.

7. O Lord, arise and enlarge the coast of my marriage, in the name of Jesus.

8. Lord Jesus, deliver my marriage from captivity, in the name of Jesus.

9. I command every enemy of my marriage to flee away forever, in the name of Jesus.

10. Every rain of affliction against my marriage, stop by force, in the name of Jesus.

11. Father Lord, deliver my marriage from pestilence, in the name of Jesus.

12. Every evil device against my marriage, die, in the name of Jesus.

13. Let the lack, poverty and sorrows in my marriage be removed forever, in the name of Jesus.

14. Any impossibility in my marriage, die, in the name of Jesus.

15. O Lord, deliver my marriage from all manner of problems, in the name of Jesus.

16. Any power that wants me to sow without reaping, be destroyed, in the name of Jesus.

17. Any evil power contending against my marriage, be disgraced, in the name of Jesus.

18. Any evil thing covered cleverly in my marriage, be exposed, in the name of Jesus.

19. I withdraw my marriage from the control of the queen of heaven, in the name of Jesus.

20. Any evil spirit that has magnified itself against God in my marriage, die, in the name of Jesus.

21. Any spirit against good confession and true repentance, die, in the name of Jesus.

22. O Lord, arise and pursue every enemy of my marriage, in the name of Jesus.

23. I command evil woes in my marriage to die, in the name of Jesus.

24. Blood of Jesus, speak peace into my marriage, in the name of Jesus.

25. I terminate any satanic war that is going on in my home, in the name of Jesus.

1. Any evil structure standing against my marriage, catch fire wherever you are, in the name of Jesus.

2. Let the resurrection power touch every dead part of my marriage, in the name of Jesus.

3. O Lord, demonstrate Your signs and wonders in my marriage, in the name of Jesus.

4. I resist the devil that has vowed to waste my marriage, in the name of Jesus.

5. Every demonic wisdom against my marriage, be turned to foolishness, in the name of Jesus.

6. Any war going on ignorantly against my marriage, be stopped, in the name of Jesus.

7. Any evil judge trying to judge my marriage, collapse and die, in the name of Jesus.

8. Any witness given against my marriage in satanic courts, be rejected, in the name of Jesus.

9. O Lord, let the enemies of my marriage be pricked in their hearts to repent, in the name of Jesus.

10. Father Lord, do a notable miracle in my marriage today, in the name of Jesus.

11. Every good door closed against my marriage, open by force, in the name of Jesus.

12. I command all true love and affections killed in my marriage to come alive, in the name of Jesus.

13. Any part of my marriage that is crippled, arise and walk by force, in the name of Jesus.

14. Let every sickness in my marriage receive divine healing, in the name of Jesus.

15. Any conversion that will favor my marriage, manifest now, in the name of Jesus.

16. Any wicked sorcerer working against my marriage, be disgraced, in the name of Jesus.

17. Let the glory of my marriage that is arrested be released by force, in the name of Jesus.

18. O Lord, command Your boldness to manifest and deliver my marriage, in the name of Jesus.

19. Any power that is fighting Christ's leadership in my marriage, die, in the name of Jesus.

20. Any evil chain holding my marriage, break to pieces, in the name of Jesus.

21. Any power contradicting God's Word in my marriage, be disgraced, in the name of Jesus.

22.   Father Lord, deliver my marriage by Yourself, in the name of Jesus.

1. Let the presence of Bar Jesus in my marriage be judged, in the name of Jesus.

2. Lord Jesus, expel every demon that is attacking my marriage, in the name of Jesus.

3. Let every helper of my marriage that is poisoned be delivered, in the name of Jesus.

4. Any flatter designed to scatter my marriage, be destroyed, in the name of Jesus.

5. Let every demon that is attacking my marriage be expelled, in the name of Jesus.

6. Any satanic assault against my marriage, be converted to honor, in the name of Jesus.

7. Every unrepentant Elymas against my marriage, receive blindness, in the name of Jesus.

8. Let the earthquake to deliver my marriage by force, in the name of Jesus.

9. Let the air quake to deliver my marriage, in the name of Jesus.

10. Let the seaquake to deliver my marriage, in the name of Jesus.

11. Let the whole creature revolt against every enemy of my marriage, in the name of Jesus.

12. Any wicked foundation that is holding my marriage, quake by force, in the name of Jesus.

13. Any kind of Iron Gate that is blocking my marriage's blessings, break open, in the name of Jesus.

14. Any power attacking my marriage at night, receive death and die, in the name of Jesus.

15. I break and loose my marriage from the attacks of the day, in the name of Jesus.

16. Every Herod that is standing against my marriage, be destroyed by divine angels, in the name of Jesus.

17. Every unrepentant enemy of my marriage, be eaten up by demonic worms, in the name of Jesus.

18. Any part of my marriage that is impotent, receive divine strength, in the name of Jesus.

19. Let divine unity and love characterize my marriage, in the name of Jesus.

20. I command every demonic judgment seat against my marriage to catch fire, in the name of Jesus.

21. Any evil power walking anywhere to destroy my marriage, be destroyed, in the name of Jesus.

22. Any evil bond against my marriage, break, in the name of Jesus.

23. Any arrow of death fired against my marriage, I fire you back, in the name of Jesus.

Day 9

1. Any evil verdict against my marriage, be revoked, in the name of Jesus.

2. Let every satanic court assigned to judge my marriage dismiss it, in the name of Jesus.

3. Every satanic storm against my marriage be calmed forever, in the name of Jesus.

4. I command every viper attacking my marriage to die, in the name of Jesus.

5. Let my marriage receive divine liberty, in the name of Jesus.

6. I command divine comfort and freedom to manifest in my marriage, in the name of Jesus.

7. Every danger ahead of my marriage, disappear by force, in the name of Jesus.

8. Let every harm done against my marriage be repaired by force, in the name of Jesus.

9. Any sickness and disease that has vowed to harvest my marriage, die, in the name of Jesus.

10. O Lord, with Your power of creation, recreate peace in my marriage, in the name of Jesus.

11. Let divine image that has departed from my marriage come back, in the name of Jesus.

12. O Lord, return my marriage to its original paradise, in the name of Jesus.

13. Let the needs of my marriage be met, in the name of Jesus.

14. O Lord, arise and visit my marriage again, in the name of Jesus.

15. Every benefit of good marriage, begin to manifest in my marriage, in the name of Jesus.

16. Father Lord, cloth my marriage with divine garment of peace and prosperity, in the name of Jesus.

17. I command my marriage to move away from curses to blessings, in the name of Jesus.

18. Father Lord, bring Your love to my marriage again, in the name of Jesus.

19. Any evil flood designed to carry my marriage, be diverted by force, in the name of Jesus.

20. O Lord, as You remembered Noah in the time of flood, remember my marriage, in the name of Jesus.

21. Father Lord, arise and scatter every enemy of my marriage, in the name of Jesus.

22.   Let my marriage receive from God lovely and godly children, in the name of Jesus.

23.   Any grudge designed to destroy my marriage, die immediately, in the name of Jesus.

1. O Lord, cause Your promised child to manifest in my marriage, in the name of Jesus.

2. Any part of Sodom and Gomorrah that has swallowed my marriage, vomit it by force, in the name of Jesus.

3. O Lord, let Your tree of my marriage grow and bear fruits, in the name of Jesus.

4. Let all the enemies of my marriage be removed from prosperity, in the name of Jesus.

5. Let my marriage receive courage and divine support to reach the end, in the name of Jesus.

6. O Lord, let the ark of my marriage be empowered to take my marriage out of dangers, in the name of Jesus.

7. Any evil soldier against my marriage, be arrested and destroyed, in the name of Jesus.

8. Anything in my marriage that has refused to glorify God, die, in the name of Jesus.

9. I command my marriage to escape from judgment of God by divine mercy, in the name of Jesus.

10.   I refuse to welcome devil into my marriage, in the name of Jesus.

11.   I command everyone in my family to refuse to listen to the devil, in the name of Jesus.

12.   My marriage will not despise God's mercy, in the name of Jesus.

13.   O Lord, defend my marriage from marriage destroyers, in the name of Jesus.

14.   O Lord, let my marriage find grace to prosper in peace, in the name of Jesus.

15.   Let every prayer offered for my marriage receive immediate answers, in the name of Jesus.

16.   O Lord, bring Your riches and abundance into my marriage, in the name of Jesus.

17.   Let every enemy of my marriage receive destructive fears, in the name of Jesus.

18.   Let the womb of my marriage open to bear many godly children, in the name of Jesus.

19.   Let the terror of God fall upon every enemy of my marriage, in the name of Jesus.

20.   Any Abimelech that has vowed to destroy my marriage, die in shame, in the name of Jesus.

21. I refuse to accept Hagar into my family, in the name of Jesus.

22. Let the spirit of barrenness be cast out of my marriage, in the name of Jesus.

1. Every Laban against my marriage, be rebuked by God, in the name of Jesus.

2. Let the arrows of wicked in-laws against my marriage backfire, in the name of Jesus.

3. Any household enemy of my marriage, be exposed and disgraced, in the name of Jesus.

4. O Lord, arise and restore my marriage to Your original plan of paradise, in the name of Jesus.

5. I command my marriage to have faith in the Lord forever, in the name of Jesus.

6. Any demonic competition going on in my family, be terminated, in the name of Jesus.

7. Any power wrestling against God in my marriage, die, in the name of Jesus.

8. Let every strange god in my family catch fire and burn to ashes, in the name of Jesus.

9. Let heaven remember my family today and bless my marriage, in the name of Jesus.

10. I command every enemy of my marriage to bow down and surrender to God, in the name of Jesus.

11. Every good dream about my marriage, be fulfilled by force, in the name of Jesus.

12. O Lord, single my marriage out and bless it exceedingly, in the name of Jesus.

13. Father Lord, arise and unite me again with my partner spiritually and physically, in the name of Jesus.

14. Let my marriage be settled in peace and in prosperity, in the name of Jesus.

15. My marriage will not be exposed to satanic attacks again, in the name of Jesus.

16. O Lord, I will not take Your grace for granted or abuse Your mercy again, in the name of Jesus.

17. I refuse to cooperate with any strange man or woman to destroy my marriage, in the name of Jesus.

18. Any garment any strange woman wants to use against me, I withdraw you, in the name of Jesus.

19. Lord Jesus, help me not to compromise my marriage for anything, in the name of Jesus.

20. Let the humility of God reign in my marriage forever, in the name of Jesus.

21. O Lord, help everyone in my family to forgive and forget, in the name of Jesus.

22. I shall not sell my birthright because of any strange man or woman, money etc, in the name of Jesus.

23. Let my marriage respect be preserved forever, in the name of Jesus.

1. My marriage will not die young, it will fulfill its purpose, in the name of Jesus.

2. Let my marriage be exalted above every worker of iniquity forever, in the name of Jesus.

3. Father Lord, spare my marriage from every evil force, in the name of Jesus.

4. O Lord, keep my marriage out of evil designers, in the name of Jesus.

5. Any satanic pestilence in my marriage, disappear, in the name of Jesus.

6. Let the love of God prevail over works of the devil in my marriage, in the name of Jesus.

7. O Lord, give my marriage favor in the sight of her enemies, in the name of Jesus.

8. Any Pharaoh that has vowed to destroy my marriage, be destroyed, in the name of Jesus.

9. Let the goodness of God dominate my marriage forever, in the name of Jesus.

10. Father Lord, remove every curse the enemy has placed upon my marriage, in the name of Jesus.

11. Let everything in my marriage surrender to the will of God by force, in the name of Jesus.

12. I command every Pharaoh of my marriage to let my marriage go, in the name of Jesus.

13. Every part of my marriage, receive the perfect fear of God, in the name of Jesus.

14. Anything in my marriage rebelling against God, surrender immediately, in the name of Jesus.

15. O Lord, heal every sick part of my marriage's destiny, in the name of Jesus.

16. Let the manna of my marriage begin to fall unhindered, in the name of Jesus.

17. O Lord, feed my marriage with the food of champions, in the name of Jesus.

18. O Lord, restore my family and keep us in peace forever, in the name of Jesus.

19. Any part of my marriage that God's blessings has abandoned, embrace blessings now, in the name of Jesus.

20. Let the spirit of borrowing that is designed to destroy my marriage die, in the name of Jesus.

21. The temple of my marriage will not be defiled, in the name of Jesus.

22. O Lord, take my marriage to her year of jubilee with every good thing, in the name of Jesus.

1. O Lord, guide and control every movement of my marriage to the Promised Land, in the name of Jesus.

2. Father Lord, deliver my marriage in times of mass marital collapse, in the name of Jesus.

3. I command my marriage to stand the test of time to fulfill its purpose, in the name of Jesus.

4. Let my marriage receive victory over all her determined enemies, in the name of Jesus.

5. You my marriage, look unto Jesus for your deliverance, in the name of Jesus.

6. Every area of my marriage that is not promoted, receive promotion now, in the name of Jesus.

7. I receive the covenant of peace for my marriage in advance, in the name of Jesus.

8. Any Balak that hired Balaam against my marriage, die without mercy, in the name of Jesus.

9. Any inherited marital shame waiting against my marriage, I reject you, in the name of Jesus.

10. I take my marriage to Jesus, the city of my refugee, in the name of Jesus.

11.   Any slayer hired to slay my marriage, die, in the name of Jesus.

12.   O Lord, arise and defend my marriage by fire, in the name of Jesus.

13.   O Lord, keep my marriage in the city of refuge forever and ever, in the name of Jesus.

14.   Any power that is meddling with my marriage, be disgraced, in the name of Jesus.

15.   I command my days of honeymoon to come back by fire, in the name of Jesus.

16.   Any evil personality removing the ancient landmark of my marriage, die, in the name of Jesus.

17.   Let that hand pushing me away from my marriage dry up by fire, in the name of Jesus.

18.   I command my marriage to abide forever in Christ, in the name of Jesus.

19.   O Lord, let my marriage begin to glorify You from now as never before, in the name of Jesus.

20.   O Lord, open the eyes of my marriage, to see the goodness of God, in the name of Jesus.

21.   Every evil spy against my marriage, die, in the name of Jesus.

22. Any Achan that has brought an accursed thing into my marriage, I reject you, in the name of Jesus.

23. Let the sun of my marriage begin to shine, in the name of Jesus.

24. If the sun or the moon must be stopped for my marriage to move forward, so be it , in the name of Jesus.

1. Any evil neighbor attacking my marriage, be exposed and disgraced, in the name of Jesus.

2. Any problem occupying any space in my marriage vacate by fire, in the name of Jesus.

3. Let all the promises of God for my marriage begin to appear, in the name of Jesus.

4. O Lord, bless my marriage even to old age, in the name of Jesus.

5. Father Lord, empower me to keep the marriage vow or covenant, in the name of Jesus.

6. Lord, give me special children that will move the world to the next level, in the name of Jesus.

7. O Lord, visit the city where I live for my sake, in the name of Jesus.

8. Any power that despises marriage, my marriage is not your candidate, in the name of Jesus.

9. O Lord, make my partner the best before me every day, in the name of Jesus.

10. Every witchcraft burden upon my marriage, drop forever, in the name of Jesus.

11. Let the voice of the Lord be heard in my family, in the name of Jesus.

12. I command woe to visit every enemy of my marriage, in the name of Jesus.

13. I separate my marriage from the midst of defeated marriages, in the name of Jesus.

14. Any evil personality busy planning against my marriage, let your brain scatter, in the name of Jesus.

15. Any wicked relative that has vowed to scatter my marriage, be disgraced, in the name of Jesus.

16. Any weapon of death raised against my marriage, destroy your owner, in the name of Jesus.

17. Any dragon sanding against my marriage, fall down flat, in the name of Jesus.

18. Any Philistine garrison warring against my marriage, die immediately, in the name of Jesus.

19. I challenge the Goliath of my marriage to die, in the name of Jesus.

20. O Lord, let everyone in my family begin to behave wisely, in the name of Jesus.

21. Let my marriage be converted to its original divine purpose, in the name of Jesus.

21 DAYS PRAYER TO KEEP YOUR MARRIAGE OUT OF TROUBLES

1.   O Lord, arise and judge every enemy of my marriage, in the name of Jesus.

2.   I command my marriage to escape every death verdict pronounce against it, in the name of Jesus.

3.   Every strange god against my marriage, I terminate your assignment, in the name of Jesus.

4.   I smite unto death every Goliath of my marriage, in the name of Jesus.

5.   Any evil neighbor that hates my marriage, be disgraced, in the name of Jesus.

6.   Let the thunder of God come down and scatter every enemy of my marriage, in the name of Jesus.

7.   O Lord, empower my marriage to escape every death plan, in the name of Jesus.

8. Father Lord, arise and preserve my marriage to the end, in the name of Jesus.

9. Any evil prayer offered against my marriage, be rejected, in the name of Jesus.

10. I command every enemy of my marriage to be restrained from evil actions, in the name of Jesus.

11. O Lord, arise and give my marriage more victories, in the name of Jesus.

12. Father Lord, deliver my marriage from fighting wrong battles, in the name of Jesus.

13. Every good thing my marriage has lost, I recover you double, in the name of Jesus.

14. O Lord, encourage me to fight the battles of my marriage, in the name of Jesus.

15. Let every satanic secret against my marriage be exposed, in the name of Jesus.

16. Every enemy of my marriage will not be spared, in the name of Jesus.

17. Let every stubborn enemy of my marriage grow weaker and weaker, in the name of Jesus.

18. I command confusion to take over the camp of my enemies, in the name of Jesus.

19. Every wicked adversary of my marriage, be disgraced by fire, in the name of Jesus.

20. O Lord, write and fight all the battles of my marriage, in the name of Jesus.

21. O Lord, release Your kindness all over my marriage, in the name of Jesus.

22. O Lord, deliver my marriage from every evil assignment, in the name of Jesus.

23. I command every enemy of my marriage to be subdued, in the name of Jesus.

Day 2

1. I recover every blessing of my marriage lost by my ancestors, in the name of Jesus.

2. Any evil revolt against my marriage, I put you to an end, in the name of Jesus.

3. O Lord, inject Your special mercy into my marriage by fire, in the name of Jesus.

4. Father Lord, hide my marriage from the reach of evil forces, in the name of Jesus.

5. Every demonic burden upon my marriage, be lifted, in the name of Jesus.

6. O Lord, help and empower me to defend my marriage with all my might, in the name of Jesus.

7. Let heaven execute judgment that will favor my marriage, in the name of Jesus.

8. Lord Jesus, bring back Your joy and happiness into my marriage, in the name of Jesus.

9. Let divine kindness begin to manifest in my marriage again, in the name of Jesus.

10. O Lord, defend my marriage's territory from evil inversion, in the name of Jesus.

11. Any evil giant that has risen against my marriage, die, in the name of Jesus.

12. O Lord, bring Your peace back in my marriage forever, in the name of Jesus.

13. Let wisdom and understanding from God enter into my home today, in the name of Jesus.

14. Let all my good heart desires for my marriage begin to manifest, in the name of Jesus.

15. I command the glory of God to appear and overshadow my marriage, in the name of Jesus.

16. Let my marriage respect and honor the God of Israel, in the name of Jesus.

17. O Lord, provide a miraculous divine apartment for my family, in the name of Jesus.

18. Father Lord, increase every good thing in my marriage to Your own glory, in the name of Jesus.

19. Every arrow of famine fired into my home, I fire you back, in the name of Jesus.

20. Let divine rains of blessing begin to fall into the garden of my marriage, in the name of Jesus.

21. Let the power that kills marriage in my environment bow and die, in the name of Jesus.

22. Any satanic army raised against my marriage, scatter, in the name of Jesus.

23. O Lord, arise and destroy the destroyers of my marriage, in the name of Jesus.

1. I command my marriage to walk out from the camp of the enemy, in the name of Jesus.

2. I stand my ground against all forces against my marriage, in the name of Jesus.

3. Let the wind of fear and destruction blow into the camp of my enemies, in the name of Jesus.

4. All enemy boasting against my marriage, be disgraced, in the name of Jesus.

5. O Lord, help me to fight all the enemies of my marriage to the end, in the name of Jesus.

6. I receive boldness to speak against the enemies of my marriage with power, in the name of Jesus.

7. I command my marriage to visit heaven and come back in victory, in the name of Jesus.

8. I receive double portion of God's Spirit to destroy the destroyers of my marriage, in the name of Jesus.

9. Any evil river flowing into the camp of my marriage, dry up, in the name of Jesus.

10. Any seed of barrenness planted in the garden of my marriage, die, in the name of Jesus.

11. Every good thing that the enemies of my marriage have killed, be resurrected now, in the name of Jesus.

12. Let all miracles that my marriage needs begin to appear, in the name of Jesus.

13. Any spiritual blindness in the destiny of my marriage, be removed, in the name of Jesus.

14. Any spiritual leprosy in the destiny of my marriage, be cleansed by the blood of Jesus, in the name of Jesus.

15. Every enemy of my marriage, be defeated unto death, in the name of Jesus.

16. O Lord, deliver my marriage from the hands of marriage killers, in the name of Jesus.

17. Let my marriage be the first to be saved from trouble, in the name of Jesus.

18. Every dry bone of my marriage, come alive by force, in the name of Jesus.

19. Let my marriage be delivered to give glory to God, in the name of Jesus.

20. Every enemy of my marriage, receive immediate judgment, in the name of Jesus.

21. Father Lord, deliver my marriage from every unnecessary war, in the name of Jesus.

22. Lord Jesus, enrich my marriage with all manner of blessings, in the name of Jesus.

1. O Lord, arise and fight for the peace of my marriage, in the name of Jesus.

2. Father Lord, open the doors of my marriage's blessings, in the name of Jesus.

3. O Lord, arise and fight every war facing my marriage, in the name of Jesus.

4. Blood of Jesus, purge my marriage and deliver it from captivity, in the name of Jesus.

5. Any satanic reign over my marriage, be terminated, in the name of Jesus.

6. Lord Jesus, bring Your reign of peace into my marriage, in the name of Jesus.

7. I command my marriage to be separated from sin, in the name of Jesus.

8. Any anti-Christ spirit attacking my marriage, be cast out, in the name of Jesus.

9. I command my marriage to walk in righteousness to the end, in the name of Jesus.

10. Any demonic spirit in the vineyard of my marriage, be cast out, in the name of Jesus.

11. O Lord, save my marriage from death, in the name of Jesus.

12. O Lord, be the sanctuary for my marriage, in the name of Jesus.

13. Father Lord, pour the water of life into my marriage today, in the name of Jesus.

14. Lord Jesus, walk my marriage out from darkness to light, in the name of Jesus.

15. Every evil reign against my marriage, be terminated by force, in the name of Jesus.

16. Blood of Jesus, bring my marriage into divine program by Your power, in the name of Jesus.

17. Blood of Jesus, help my marriage to go as God commanded from the beginning, in the name of Jesus.

18. Let every aspect of my marriage respond to God's demands, in the name of Jesus.

19. Any evil plot to arrest the star of my marriage, fail woefully, in the name of Jesus.

20. O Lord, reverse every curse ever pronounced against my marriage, in the name of Jesus.

21. Let my marriage be delivered from every manner of death, in the name of Jesus.

22. Let every evil plan against my marriage be revealed and destroyed, in the name of Jesus.

23. Father Lord, assign the angels of heaven to build my marriage, in the name of Jesus.

1. I command my marriage to be freed from every manner of bondage, in the name of Jesus.

2. O Lord, arise and punish every enemy of my marriage, in the name of Jesus.

3. Every manner of sickness, diseases and problems, depart from my marriage, in the name of Jesus.

4. Any arrow of paralysis fired into my marriage, I fire you back, in the name of Jesus.

5. Any part of my marriage that is possessed, receive deliverance, in the name of Jesus.

6. I command every attack against my marriage from the tomb to die, in the name of Jesus.

7. Every fierce demon tormenting my marriage, be cast out, in the name of Jesus.

8. Any satanic roadblock that was mounted for the sake of my marriage, be dismantled, in the name of Jesus.

9. You the eyes of my marriage, open, in the name of Jesus.

10. Any power from the sea attacking my marriage, be destroyed, in the name of Jesus.

11. Any demonic spirit vexing my marriage, be cast out, in the name of Jesus.

12. Let the demons attacking my life from fire be disgraced, in the name of Jesus.

13. Any unclean spirit, polluting my marriage, be destroyed, in the name of Jesus.

14. Let the hand of Christ touch my sick marriage today for deliverance, in the name of Jesus.

15. O Lord, move into my marriage with Your compassion and heal it, in the name of Jesus.

16. Father Lord, guide my marriage across the rivers of life, in the name of Jesus.

17. Any power that has defiled my marriage's garment, die, in the name of Jesus.

18. O Lord, cleanse my garment and make it clean by the blood of Jesus, in the name of Jesus.

19. Let the miracle that will reposition my marriage appear by force, in the name of Jesus.

20. Any water spirit fish that has swallowed my marriage's finance, vomit it now, in the name of Jesus.

21. Any demonic rock that has arrested my marriage, release it by force, in the name of Jesus.

22. Let spirits in the grave be tormented to release my marriage, in the name of Jesus.

Day 6

1. Every diverse spirit attacking my marriage, be arrested unto death, in the name of Jesus.

2. Any evil force that has plagued my marriage, be frustrated, in the name of Jesus.

3. Let the storms assigned to waste my marriage be wasted, in the name of Jesus.

4. Every contrary wind blowing against my marriage, be diverted, in the name of Jesus.

5. You my marriage under torment of death, receive abundant life, in the name of Jesus.

6. Any evil power drinking the blood of my marriage, shut your mouth and die, in the name of Jesus.

7. O Lord, appear in the battlefield and deliver my marriage, in the name of Jesus.

8. You my dead marriage, hear the voice of resurrection and arise, in the name of Jesus.

9. You the evil spirit in my marriage, hold your peace and come out by force, in the name of Jesus.

10. Every evil mouth speaking against my marriage, close forever and ever, in the name of Jesus.

11. Every sin empowering my marriage's problems, I break your backbone, in the name of Jesus.

12. I command my marriage to touch Lord Jesus Christ by faith, in the name of Jesus.

13. Any part of my marriage that is disabled, receive deliverance, in the name of Jesus.

14. Let every spirit of impediment in my marriage be cast out now, in the name of Jesus.

15. Let the tree of my marriage begin to bear fruits, in the name of Jesus.

16. You my marriage, be of good cheer and receive your total deliverance, in the name of Jesus.

17. Let every problem in my marriage cease by force, in the name of Jesus.

18. Every spirit of toiling in my marriage, die, in the name of Jesus.

19. The labors of my marriage will not be in vain, in the name of Jesus.

20. You my marriage, weep not, rise and shine, in the name of Jesus.

21. Let the finished wine of my marriage be restored by Christ, in the name of Jesus.

22. Any spirit of polygamy coming into my marriage, I disgrace you out, in the name of Jesus.

23. O Lord, bless my marriage financially, in the name of Jesus.

24. O Lord, let my marriage be filled with respect, in the name of Jesus.

1. Every yoke of polygamy in my marriage, break and lose your hold, in the name of Jesus.

2. O Lord, if my marriage is in a wrong place, take it to the right place, in the name of Jesus.

3. Father Lord, blow Your trumpet of jubilee in my marriage, in the name of Jesus.

4. Let the movement of my marriage be controlled by God, in the name of Jesus.

5. Every effect of my mistakes in marriage, receive deliverance, in the name of Jesus.

6. Every unclean desire polluting my marriage, be destroyed, in the name of Jesus.

7. Any evil offering on evil altar against my marriage, expire, in the name of Jesus.

8. I refuse the enticement of any strange man or woman, in the name of Jesus.

9. Unchangeable God, change every evil situation in my family, in the name of Jesus.

10. Every blessing of my marriage stolen by strange man or woman, be restored, in the name of Jesus.

11. Let the death of Jesus deliver my marriage from bondage, in the name of Jesus.

12. O Lord, arise and move my marriage forward, in the name of Jesus.

13. Any power assigned to return my marriage to Egypt, die, in the name of Jesus.

14. Let the truth that will get my marriage free be exposed, in the name of Jesus.

15. Every decision taking against my marriage, be reversed, in the name of Jesus.

16. Let righteousness begin to reign in my marriage, in the name of Jesus.

17. Every evil unity against my marriage, scatter, in the name of Jesus.

18. Let the language of the enemies of my marriage be confounded, in the name of Jesus.

19. Father Lord, rescue my marriage from destruction, in the name of Jesus.

20. O Lord, arise and comfort me with Your blessings in my marriage, in the name of Jesus.

21. Let my marriage receive the grace of God to entertain angels, in the name of Jesus.

22. I command my marriage to come out from Sodom and Gomorrah, in the name of Jesus.

23. Any evil king that has captured my marriage, release it, in the name of Jesus.

Day 8

1. Any sin keeping my marriage in bondage, be confused and destroyed, in the name of Jesus.

2. I receive power to do any restitution that will set my marriage free, in the name of Jesus.

3. O Lord, help me to pay any price to set my family free from bondage, in the name of Jesus.

4. Any war going on against my marriage because of my mistakes, be terminated, in the name of Jesus.

5. Let every unfulfilled dream for my marriage begin to manifest, in the name of Jesus.

6. Every unsettled case in my marriage, be settled by force, in the name of Jesus.

7. Anything my in-laws are using against my marriage, be destroyed by the blood of Jesus, in the name of Jesus.

8. Any evil dedication attacking my marriage, be revoked, in the name of Jesus.

9. Every unfulfilled promise troubling my marriage, lose your hold, in the name of Jesus.

10. Every sad situation troubling my marriage, receive solution, in the name of Jesus.

11. Any household enemy ready to waste my marriage, fail woefully, in the name of Jesus.

12. I remove every strange god in my family by force, in the name of Jesus.

13. O Lord, release my marriage from the control of the wicked, in the name of Jesus.

14. Blood of Jesus, silence every innocent blood crying against my marriage, in the name of Jesus.

15. Any Goliath that is destroying my family, received final destruction, in the name of Jesus.

16. O Lord, turn around every captivity in my marriage, in the name of Jesus.

17. Father Lord, take my marriage to a place of rest and peace, in the name of Jesus.

18. I command divine favor to begin to manifest in my marriage, in the name of Jesus.

19. Any evil power ridiculing my marriage, be disgraced, in the name of Jesus.

20. O Lord, give my marriage victory against all odds, in the name of Jesus.

21. Let every enemy of my marriage be defeated in battle, in the name of Jesus.

22. O Lord, let Your purpose for my marriage be fulfilled, in the name of Jesus.

23. Father Lord, provide everything my marriage will ever need, in the name of Jesus.

24. I drive affliction far away from my family, in the name of Jesus.

25. Every demonic agent assigned to trouble my family, be aborted, in the name of Jesus.

26. Blood of Jesus, envelop my marriage with Your divine peace, in the name of Jesus.

27. Every evil verdict against my marriage, be reversed by force, in the name of Jesus.

28. Let my marriage receive wisdom to overcome every problem, in the name of Jesus.

29. Any demon against my marriage, be cast out, in the name of Jesus.

30. Every spirit of rebellion attacking my marriage, be frustrated, in the name of Jesus.

31. I command healing and deliverance upon my wounded marriage, in the name of Jesus.

32. I withdraw my marriage from the influence of wrong association, in the name of Jesus.

33. Every darkness upon my marriage, be swallowed by divine light, in the name of Jesus.

34. Father Lord, move my marriage from minimum to maximum, in the name of Jesus.

35. Any evil personality that has swallowed joy in my marriage, vomit it, in the name of Jesus.

36. I receive the anointing to fulfill every good vision I have for my marriage, in the name of Jesus.

37. Father Lord, lead me to take the right steps that will deliver my marriage, in the name of Jesus.

38. Blood of Jesus, take my marriage to the Promised Land, in the name of Jesus.

39. I open every door of progress closed against my marriage, in the name of Jesus.

40. Father Lord, lead me into the path that will set my marriage free, in the name of Jesus.

41. Anything that need to die for my marriage to live, die, in the name of Jesus.

42. Every demonic storm attacking my marriage, be calmed, in the name of Jesus.

43. Every evil mark of trouble against my marriage, be cleansed by the blood of Jesus, in the name of Jesus.

44. Any strongman that has vowed to kill my marriage, die by fire, in the name of Jesus.

45. Any evil foundation built against my marriage, collapse, in the name of Jesus.

1. Let darkness overtake the enemies of my marriage, in the name of Jesus.

2. Any satanic regulation against my marriage, scatter, in the name of Jesus.

3. Any demon on assignment to destroy my marriage, be destroyed, in the name of Jesus.

4. Let spiritual blindness cover the eyes of the enemies of my marriage, in the name of Jesus.

5. Father Lord, empower my marriage to escape the grip of marriage destroyers, in the name of Jesus.

6. O Lord, empower my marriage to fulfill its goal by fire, in the name of Jesus.

7. I command my marriage to begin to magnetize divine blessings, in the name of Jesus.

8. Every enemy of my marital breakthrough, die by fire, in the name of Jesus.

9. Every seed of failure planted against my marriage, die, in the name of Jesus.

10. Every dark force militating against my marriage, scatter, in the name of Jesus.

11. O Lord, cause my marriage to be too hot to be dissolved by the enemy, in the name of Jesus.

12. Every satanic padlock against my destiny, break to pieces, in the name of Jesus.

13. Any power that has vowed to kill my marriage prematurely, die, in the name of Jesus.

14. Any evil genius working against my marriage, be frustrated to death, in the name of Jesus.

15. Every yoke of marital breakup upon my marriage, break, in the name of Jesus.

16. Any power that has vowed to stop my marriage half way, die, in the name of Jesus.

17. O Lord, feed my marriage with heavenly manner to prevail, in the name of Jesus.

18. Blood of Jesus, speak death unto every enemy of my marriage, in the name of Jesus.

19. Any satanic giant holding my marriage to ransom, be destroyed, in the name of Jesus.

20. Every yoke of prayerlessness against my marriage, break, in the name of Jesus.

21. Every arrow of disagreement fired against my marriage, I fire you back, in the name of Jesus.

22. I deliver my marriage from the forces of hell fire, in the name of Jesus.

1. Any evil spirit that has possessed my marriage, be cast out by force, in the name of Jesus.

2. Any dark force assigned to swallow my marriage, be swallowed by death, in the name of Jesus.

3. Every opportunity that the devil and his agents have stolen from my marriage be released, in the name of Jesus.

4. Let the power of the Holy Ghost bring back every happy moment I have lost, in the name of Jesus.

5. Any power that wants my marriage to fall apart, be harvested by death, in the name of Jesus.

6. Every secret that will deliver my marriage, begin to manifest, in the name of Jesus.

7. The problems in my marriage will not confuse me, in the name of Jesus.

8. Any power that wants me to surrender must die in shame, in the name of Jesus.

9. Any marital problem that is already frustrating me, be frustrated, in the name of Jesus.

10. Any power causing me to be tired of my marriage, die immediately, in the name of Jesus.

11. O Lord, respond quickly and deliver my marriage from death, in the name of Jesus.

12. O Lord, treat my marriage as an emergency case, in the name of Jesus.

13. Let heavenly soldiers arise to support my marriage, in the name of Jesus.

14. Every weapon of marital collapse being used against my marriage, fail, in the name of Jesus.

15. O Lord, give my marriage a quick spiritual help, in the name of Jesus.

16. Let the sacrifice of our Lord Jesus save my marriage from collapse, in the name of Jesus.

17. Every evil wall built against my marriage, collapse by thunder, in the name of Jesus.

18. Father Lord, help me to fulfill my responsibility in this marriage, in the name of Jesus.

19. Any power sinking the boat of my marriage, die, in the name of Jesus.

20. Let every evil power moving my marriage from peace die, in the name of Jesus.

21. O Lord, take my marriage to its right place, in the name of Jesus.

22. Blood of Jesus, speak my marriage out of death, in the name of Jesus.

1. Every inherited limitation upon my marriage, disappear, in the name of Jesus.

2. Any manipulation going on against my marriage, be terminated, in the name of Jesus.

3. Every dangerous danger against my marriage, be destroyed, in the name of Jesus.

4. Any problem that has swallowed God's promise for my marriage, be wasted, in the name of Jesus.

5. Let divine hail stone fall upon the head of my marital problems, in the name of Jesus.

6. Let every Egyptian that is against my marriage die in the Red Sea, in the name of Jesus.

7. Any serpent of poverty in my marriage, die by force, in the name of Jesus.

8. O Lord, deliver my marriage from demonic stagnancy, in the name of Jesus.

9. I take authority over every enemy of my marriage, in the name of Jesus.

10. Every inheritance belonging to my marriage that is in the hands of the enemy, I recover you, in the name of Jesus.

11. I command the powers of the queen of heaven to release my marriage, in the name of Jesus.

12. O Lord, arise and perform a miracle that will set my marriage free, in the name of Jesus.

13. Blessed Holy Spirit, fill my marriage with Your power, in the name of Jesus.

14. O Lord, help me to relate very well with my life partner, in the name of Jesus.

15. Every good thing my marriage has ever conceived, be delivered without delay, in the name of Jesus.

16. O Lord, arise and guide my marriage to the highest level, in the name of Jesus.

17. Let the resurrection power quicken every dead area of my marriage, in the name of Jesus.

18. Holy Spirit, arise and make my marriage holy, in the name of Jesus.

19. Let the Spirit of God fill my marriage with power from above, in the name of Jesus.

20. Let the Spirit of Christ possess my marriage by force, in the name of Jesus.

21. Let the Spirit of truth rule and reign over my marriage, in the name of Jesus.

22. O Lord, take my marriage to Your destination, in the name of Jesus.

23. Let my marriage receive open heaven, in the name of Jesus.

1. Let the eternal Spirit give my marriage power to succeed forever, in the name of Jesus.

2. By the power of the omnipotent God, I command my marriage to move forward, in the name of Jesus.

3. Let the oil of the Holy Ghost drop down from heavens upon my marriage, in the name of Jesus.

4. Let the water of life cleanse my marriage from pollutions, in the name of Jesus.

5. Any evil wind blowing into my marriage, be removed, in the name of Jesus.

6. Let the fire of God burn to ashes every enemy of my marriage, in the name of Jesus.

7. O Lord, arise and seal my marriage with Holy Ghost seal, in the name of Jesus.

8. Every evil heart against my marriage, be purged by the Holy Ghost, in the name of Jesus.

9. O Lord, convict every enemy of my marriage to repent, in the name of Jesus.

10. Father Lord, arise and regenerate my marriage to Your own glory, in the name of Jesus.

11. Father Lord, adopt my marriage into Your heavenly family, in the name of Jesus.

12. Every deep secret that will deliver my marriage from troubles, manifest, in the name of Jesus.

13. Blessed Holy Spirit, help my marriage in prayer, in the name of Jesus.

14. Lord Jesus, create peace into my marriage by Your power, in the name of Jesus.

15. Let the power from above rescue my marriage from every trouble, in the name of Jesus.

16. Let my marriage become thirsty for true deliverance, in the name of Jesus.

17. Every enemy of deliverance in my marriage, be disgraced, in the name of Jesus.

18. Every filthiness in my marriage, be cleansed by the blood of Jesus, in the name of Jesus.

19. Let the idol assigned to waste my marriage be uprooted by death, in the name of Jesus.

20. O Lord, give everyone in my family a new heart, in the name of Jesus.

21. Blood of Jesus, circumcise the hearts of everyone in my family, in the name of Jesus.

22. Let my marital problems bow to the deliverance power of God, in the name of Jesus.

Day 13

1. Let the discerning Spirit of God discern and destroy every enemy of my marriage, in the name of Jesus.

2. I command divine miracle to take place in my marriage by force, in the name of Jesus.

3. Let every counterfeit troubling my marriage be wasted, in the name of Jesus.

4. O Lord, pump Your grace into my marriage for deliverance, in the name of Jesus.

5. Let the power of God bring discipline and purity into my marriage, in the name of Jesus.

6. O Lord, command the nine fruits of the Spirit to come alive in my marriage, in the name of Jesus.

7. Let healing and holiness capture every aspect of my marriage, in the name of Jesus.

8. Let the mercy of God fall upon my marriage by fire, in the name of Jesus.

9. O Lord, command every tongue in my family to be bridled, in the name of Jesus.

10. Let divine inspiration inspire my marriage for true deliverance, in the name of Jesus.

11. I command the spirit of liberty to flow into the root of my marriage, in the name of Jesus.

12. Let the excellent spirit from above enter into my family today, in the name of Jesus.

13. O Lord, arise and renew Your power in my marriage, in the name of Jesus.

14. O Lord, give my marriage a sound, divine and motivating principles, in the name of Jesus.

15. Let the purpose of every heart in my family be saintly motivated, in the name of Jesus.

16. Let every soul in my family begin to search for purity, in the name of Jesus.

17. Let the supernatural power of God enter into my marriage today, in the name of Jesus.

18. Let peace reign in my family as from today by God's grace, in the name of Jesus.

19. O Lord, renew and mature every heart in my family, in the name of Jesus.

20. Let my life partner and me yield to the will of God, in the name of Jesus.

21. I command my marriage to be unlocked, in the name of Jesus.

22. I walk my marriage out of demonic dark rooms, in the name of Jesus.

Day 14

1. O Lord, arise and give my marriage open heaven, in the name of Jesus.

2. Let all the evil forces in the heavenlies against my marriage scatter, in the name of Jesus.

3. Every satanic checkpoint that has arrested my marriage, release it, in the name of Jesus.

4. I release my marriage from evil spiritual lockup, in the name of Jesus.

5. Any unprofitable delays against my marriage, be lifted by fire, in the name of Jesus.

6. Let every evil exposure against my marriage be frustrated, in the name of Jesus.

7. Every demonic accusation against my marriage, be disengaged, in the name of Jesus.

8. Every evil protest and riot against my marriage, be disengaged, in the name of Jesus.

9. Let every spiritual accident against my marriage die in the spirit, in the name of Jesus.

10. Any power that has caged the destiny of my marriage, die, in the name of Jesus.

11. O Lord, arise and deliver my marriage from every evil arrest, in the name of Jesus.

12. Let every part of my marriage begin to submit to the scriptures, in the name of Jesus.

13. Any evil power fighting against God's Word in my marriage, die, in the name of Jesus.

14. Father Lord, give my marriage an uninterrupted peace and victory, in the name of Jesus.

15. Let my marriage give royalty and supreme love to God's Word, in the name of Jesus.

16. Let the intense desire to know God more begin to reign in my marriage, in the name of Jesus.

17. Let the consuming love for truth reign in my marriage, in the name of Jesus.

18. Let everyone in my family learn to spend time with God's Word, in the name of Jesus.

19. O Lord, help my family to receive open heaven and maintain it, in the name of Jesus.

20. I refuse to carry a cross that is not meant for me, in the name of Jesus.

21. O Lord, help me to carry my cross daily following Christ, in the name of Jesus.

22. I refuse to avoid any battle I must fight to enjoy my marriage, in the name of Jesus.

1. Any evil power harvesting people's marriages, I cast you out of my marriage, in the name of Jesus.

2. My marriage will not be an evil case study, in the name of Jesus.

3. Any spiritual soldier from the waters militating against my marriage, be disgraced, in the name of Jesus.

4. Any evil personality that has vowed to make my marriage a victim of divorce, die, in the name of Jesus.

5. Any decision taken anywhere against my marriage, fail woefully, in the name of Jesus.

6. I command every occult group against my marriage to scatter, in the name of Jesus.

7. Let every trap of sexual perversion designed to waste my marriage fail, in the name of Jesus.

8. Any evil information spreading like wild fire to scatter my marriage, be arrested, in the name of Jesus.

9. Any attack from the grave against my marriage, fail woefully, in the name of Jesus.

10. I refuse to make any mistake that will destroy my marriage, in the name of Jesus.

11. O Lord, deliver my marriage from any sin in the past, in the name of Jesus.

12. O Lord, help me to take the right steps to deliver my marriage, in the name of Jesus.

13. I break and loose my marriage from problems of parental sins, in the name of Jesus.

14. Wherever they have called my marriage for evil, Lord Jesus, answer for me, in the name of Jesus.

15. Any evil summon designed to destroy my marriage, die by fire, in the name of Jesus.

16. Let soul hunters that are after my marriage be disgraced, in the name of Jesus.

17. O Lord, take away my marriage from strange places, in the name of Jesus.

18. Any satanic dream that has tampered with my marriage, die, in the name of Jesus.

19. Any problem in my marriage that is making me to be fed up with life, die in the name of Jesus.

20. O Lord, renew Your blessings that have expired in my marriage, in the name of Jesus.

1. Any witch or wizard on assignment to turn the table of my marriage, die, in the name of Jesus.

2. Any evil personality that wants to kill my marriage to renew his or her own, fail woefully, in the name of Jesus.

3. Whosoever must perish for my marriage to survive, perish, in the name of Jesus.

4. Any evil and unrepentant brain planning against my marriage, receive madness, in the name of Jesus.

5. Let evil groups with all manners of evil spirits against my marriage be disengaged, in the name of Jesus.

6. Let demons on special assignment against my marriage destroy their sender, in the name of Jesus.

7. Any oppression going on against my marriage, be reversed, in the name of Jesus.

8. Any evil exchange going on against my marriage, be terminated, in the name of Jesus.

9. Any marital problem designed to destroy my faith in Christ, die, in the name of Jesus.

10. Let every deception and apostasy that is already in my marriage be frustrated, in the name of Jesus.

11. Any power modifying the Word of God to waste my marriage, be wasted, in the name of Jesus.

12. O Lord, let my marriage be empowered to please You alone, in the name of Jesus.

13. Any evil influence in my marriage desiring quick and evil riches, die, in the name of Jesus.

14. I command every man made goal attacking my marriage to be abandoned, in the name of Jesus.

15. Let the spirit of inability to accept one's fault in my marriage die, in the name of Jesus.

16. Any influence of pressure group in my environment warring against my marriage, be frustrated, in the name of Jesus.

17. I command all the carnal people in my marriage to be dispersed, in the name of Jesus.

18. Any crave for evil popularity attacking my family, be cast out of my marriage, in the name of Jesus.

19. O Lord, help my marriage not to lose the victory it has already gained, in the name of Jesus.

20. My marriage will not lose its favor , in the name of Jesus.

21. Let divine security and protection surround my marriage forever, in the name of Jesus.

22. Any problem in my marriage attacking my ministry, life and eternity, die, in the name of Jesus.

1. Every confirmed enemy of my marriage, die and die again, in the name of Jesus.

2. Any evil power standing between me and my life partner, die, in the name of Jesus.

3. Let the powers of darkness exposing my marriage to death die, in the name of Jesus.

4. Every broken wall in my marriage, be rebuilt by force, in the name of Jesus.

5. Every arrow of death and destruction fired against my marriage, backfire, in the name of Jesus.

6. I release my enslaved marriage from marriage destroyers, in the name of Jesus.

7. I command death and destruction to leave my marriage alone forever, in the name of Jesus.

8. I resist unto death every evil power against my marriage, in the name of Jesus.

9. I break and loose my marriage from the grips of foundational bondage, in the name of Jesus.

10. Any wall of relationship broken in my marriage, be rebuilt, in the name of Jesus.

11. Any power that has destroyed my marriage's family altar, die, in the name of Jesus.

12. O Lord, restore my practice of praying with my life partner, in the name of Jesus.

13. Any evil gap between me and my life partner, be closed by Christ, in the name of Jesus.

14. Any sin that has broken the walls of my marriage, die, in the name of Jesus.

15. O Lord, impart into my life and my life partner forgiven spirit, in the name of Jesus.

16. Let every difference between me and my life partner be forgotten by fire, in the name of Jesus.

17. Every un-built wall in my marriage, be built by force, in the name of Jesus.

18. Any power working against my marriage, be disgraced forever, in the name of Jesus.

19. Every cankerworm and caterpillar against my marriage, die, in the name of Jesus.

20. Let the fire of enemies of my marriage quench, in the name of Jesus.

21. O Lord, restore my relationship with my life partner, in the name of Jesus.

22. Let the true love for marriage return double into my marriage, in the name of Jesus.

1. Any special altar built against my marriage, catch fire and burn to ashes, in the name of Jesus.

2. Any witchcraft altar planned against my marriage, be dismantled, in the name of Jesus.

3. O Lord, show me how to come out of my marriage problems, in the name of Jesus.

4. Any witchcraft food prepared against my marriage, I reject you, in the name of Jesus.

5. Every spirit of depression and rejection troubling my marriage, be cast out, in the name of Jesus.

6. Let every good thing the enemy has deprived my married be recovered, in the name of Jesus.

7. Any arrow of disaster fired against my marriage, backfire, in the name of Jesus.

8. Any suicide spirit that has refused to let my marriage go, die alone, in the name of Jesus.

9. Let every menstrual manipulation going on against my marriage die, in the name of Jesus.

10. Every evil link bringing my marriage and her enemies together, be blocked, in the name of Jesus.

11. I command every unexplainable problem in my life to die mysteriously, in the name of Jesus.

12. I confront and conquer every enemy of my marriage, in the name of Jesus.

13. Every yoke of hardship and suffering against my marriage, break, in the name of Jesus.

14. Every pain the enemy has ever caused my marriage, be destroyed, in the name of Jesus.

15. Any negative medical report working against my marriage, die, in the name of Jesus.

16. Every satanic habit working hard to destroy my marriage, die, in the name of Jesus.

17. Any invisible barrier standing against my marriage, be dismantled, in the name of Jesus.

18. Every arrow of backwardness fired against my marriage, I fire you back, in the name of Jesus.

19. Every problem in my marriage causing me sleepless nights, die, in the name of Jesus.

20. Any evil character attacking the foundation of my marriage hard, be destroyed, in the name of Jesus.

21. Let every uncontrollable evil action attacking my marriage die, in the name of Jesus.

22. Any seasonal problem attacking my marriage at weak moments, die, in the name of Jesus.

1. Every uncompromising addiction and chronic problem against my marriage, die, in the name of Jesus.

2. Every seasonal attacks against my marriage, I terminate your work, in the name of Jesus.

3. Any arrow of miscarriage and evil plantation in my marriage, die, in the name of Jesus.

4. Any strange movement against my marriage, be demobilized, in the name of Jesus.

5. O Lord, deliver my marriage from financial insufficiency, in the name of Jesus.

6. Any stubborn pursuer of my marriage, fall down and die, in the name of Jesus.

7. Every yoke of terrible marriage instability in my life, break, in the name of Jesus.

8. I break and loose my marriage from spirit husband and wife, in the name of Jesus.

9. Any vagabond and fugitive mark upon my marriage, break, in the name of Jesus.

10. Any power that has diverted love away from my marriage, die, in the name of Jesus.

11. O Lord, restore everything that will make my marriage to work, in the name of Jesus.

12. Let every seducing spirit that is working against my marriage die, in the name of Jesus.

13. I command every spirit of agony upon my marriage to be cast out, in the name of Jesus.

14. Let every magician against my marriage be disgraced, in the name of Jesus.

15. Every organized darkness against my marriage, scatter by fire, in the name of Jesus.

16. Every sexual demon of incest and sexual perversion against my marriage, die, in the name of Jesus.

17. Let that spirit in my marriage that swallows progress, die, in the name of Jesus.

18. I speak to my marriage from heaven and I command deliverance to take place, in the name of Jesus.

19. Arrows of marital failure presently on my marriage, disappear, in the name of Jesus.

20. You my marriage receive divine visitation today, in the name of Jesus.

1. Let the angels of God arise and shoot enemies of my marriage at sight, in the name of Jesus.

2. Every lion in the garden of my marriage, die, in the name of Jesus.

3. Every death decree against my marriage, be reversed, in the name of Jesus.

4. I command the Samuel of my marriage to appear by fire, in the name of Jesus.

5. Let fire come down from heaven against the enemies of my marriage, in the name of Jesus.

6. I command the coast of my marriage to be enlarged by fire, in the name of Jesus.

7. Let the Haman of my marriage die, in the name of Jesus.

8. Anything that is troubling my marriage, be troubled unto death, in the name of Jesus.

9. Any serpent of darkness biting my marriage, die, in the name of Jesus.

10. O Lord, arise and deliver my marriage in times of troubles, in the name of Jesus.

11. O Lord, arise and deliver my marriage in times of sickness and confusion, in the name of Jesus.

12. Let every evil threat against my marriage be destroyed, in the name of Jesus.

13. O Lord, deliver my marriage from homeless situations, in the name of Jesus.

14. Father Lord, deliver my marriage from suffering and witchcraft attacks, in the name of Jesus.

15. O Lord, deliver my marriage from agents of mockery, in the name of Jesus.

16. O Lord, deliver my marriage from the hands of marriage wasters, in the name of Jesus.

17. Every marital turbulence against my marriage, be destroyed, in the name of Jesus.

18. Every destructive yoke of poverty in my marriage, break to pieces, in the name of Jesus.

19. Any evil seed invested in the garden of my marriage, die, in the name of Jesus.

20. Any power that wants my marriage to die painful death in silence, die, in the name of Jesus.

21. My marriage will no longer meet wrong people, in the name of Jesus.

22. O Lord, raise divine helpers to help my marriage out of troubles, in the name of Jesus.

1. Every contrary power against my marriage, be disgraced, in the name of Jesus.

2. I command every marriage hijacker against my marriage to be frustrated, in the name of Jesus.

3. Holy Ghost fire, incubate my marriage, in the name of Jesus.

4. I cast out every spirit of disunity in my marriage, in the name of Jesus.

5. Any problem that has vowed to harvest my marriage, die, in the name of Jesus.

6. Blood of Jesus speak peace and progress into my marriage, in the name of Jesus.

7. Let divine wall be constructed round about my marriage, in the name of Jesus.

8. Every hindrance to my marital breakthrough, be removed, in the name of Jesus.

9. Let the spirit of conjugal love possess my marriage by fire, in the name of Jesus.

10. Any blessing that has deserted my marriage, return back double, in the name of Jesus.

11. Every hold of the wicked against my marriage, be broken, in the name of Jesus.

12. Every problem that entered into my marriage the day I wedded, die, in the name of Jesus.

13. Any curse ever placed against my marriage by anyone dead or alive, expire, in the name of Jesus.

14. Ancient of days, bring Your Spirit into my marriage, in the name of Jesus.

15. Let my honeymoon return and depart no more, in the name of Jesus.

16. Every messenger of the devil against my marriage, carry your message to your sender, in the name of Jesus.

17. Any evil power sponsoring problems in my marriage, be disgraced, in the name of Jesus.

18. Father Lord, deliver me from every marital problems, in the name of Jesus.

19. Any poison in my marriage, spiritually or physically, die, in the name of Jesus.

20. Every bad report against my marriage, be converted to testimony, in the name of Jesus.

21. O Lord, arise and deliver me from marital failure, in the name of Jesus.

40 DAYS PRAYER TO KEEP YOUR MARRIAGE OUT OF TROUBLES

1. Every invitation given to the enemy into my marriage, I withdraw you now, in the name of Jesus.

2. Every property of the enemy in my marriage, be destroyed, in the name of Jesus.

3. Any evil invested by my ancestors in my marriage, catch fire, in the name of Jesus.

4. Any inherited marital problem in my family, I destroy you by fire, in the name of Jesus.

5. O Lord, arise and deliver my marriage from captivity, in the name of Jesus.

6. Every evil force attacking my marriage, scatter, in the name of Jesus.

7. Any evil voice speaking against my marriage, be silenced forever, in the name of Jesus.

8. Blood of Jesus, rescue my marriage from ancient demons, in the name of Jesus.

9. Any power that has made my marriage a traitor, die, in the name of Jesus.

10. Any power that has made my marriage outcast before God, die, in the name of Jesus.

11. I release my marriage from the captivity of the devil, in the name of Jesus.

12. O Lord, do not forsake my marriage, in the mighty name of Jesus.

13. Every leprosy in any part of my marriage, be cleansed, in the name of Jesus.

14. Every good thing that has abandoned my marriage, begin to come back now, in the name of Jesus.

15. Every satanic attack against my marriage be terminated, in the name of Jesus.

16. O Lord, write my marriage in the book of Your remembrance, in the name of Jesus.

17. Let everything that is against my marriage be disgraced, in the name of Jesus.

18. O Lord, do not forsake my marriage, in the name of Jesus.

19. O Lord, remove Your wrath from my marriage, in the name of Jesus.

20. I command the wrath of the enemies of my marriage to disappear, in the name of Jesus.

21. O Lord, do not cast out my marriage from Your presence, in the name of Jesus.

22. Let heaven remember my marriage, in the mighty name of Jesus.

23. Let the resurrection power quicken my marriage to life, in the name of Jesus.

24. Father Lord, by Your mercy and power walk back into my marriage, in the name of Jesus.

1. Let the Spirit of life from God enter into my marriage today, in the name of Jesus.

2. O Lord, hid my marriage from the wrath of the enemy, in the name of Jesus.

3. Every demonic attack against my marriage, come to an end, in the name of Jesus.

4. O Lord, help me to receive Your mercy and presence again, in the name of Jesus.

5. Every sickness in my marriage, spiritual and physical, receive divine healing, in the name of Jesus.

6. Any evil power terrorizing my marriage, die by force, in the name of Jesus.

7. I command every shame upon my marriage to be destroyed, in the name of Jesus.

8. Let all impossibilities in my marriage be converted to possibilities, in the name of Jesus.

9. Every satanic enslavement in my marriage, be destroyed, in the name of Jesus.

10. I release my marriage from sorrow and afflictions of the enemy, in the name of Jesus.

11. I break and loose my marriage from powers of eternal punishment, in the name of Jesus.

12. I command any voice of sin in my marriage to be silenced, in the name of Jesus.

13. Blood of Jesus, speak my marriage out of powers of sin, in the name of Jesus.

14. Let the full presence of God return back double to my marriage, in the name of Jesus.

15. O Lord, channel Your streams of mercy back to my marriage, in the name of Jesus.

16. Let the anointing of God flow into my marriage and break every evil yoke, in the name of Jesus.

17. My marriage will not compromise with my enemies again, in the name of Jesus.

18. Every seed of covetousness in my marriage, be uprooted by fire, in the name of Jesus.

19. I deliver my marriage from every evil influence of the society, in the name of Jesus.

20. Let the fire of God judge every spirit of fear in my marriage, in the name of Jesus.

21. Let pride and arrogance in my marriage be uprooted by fire, in the name of Jesus.

22. I command the love of money and worldliness to die in my marriage, in the name of Jesus.

23. Any law of the nation that contradicts God's Word in my marriage, die, in the name of Jesus.

1. Let the spirit of boasting and self confidence be cast out of my marriage, in the name of Jesus.

2. O Lord, restore Your first love into my family with Your peace, in the name of Jesus.

3. Let the true light of God begin to shine brighter in my marriage, in the name of Jesus.

4. Any power that wants my marriage to turn back to sin, die, in the name of Jesus.

5. I command all little foxes that have risen against my marriage to die, in the name of Jesus.

6. Let the spiritual life and strength of my marriage increase, in the name of Jesus.

7. Every arrow of weakness in my marriage, backfire, in the name of Jesus.

8. Any flesh that has gained supremacy over the Spirit of God in my marriage, die, in the name of Jesus.

9. Let no one misuse his or her rights in my family again, in the name of Jesus.

10. Let light from the Word of God rule, reign and control my marriage, in the name of Jesus.

11. Every spirit of unbelief in my marriage, I cast you out, in the name of Jesus.

12. O Lord, restore the Spirit of prayer and spiritual warfare in my marriage, in the name of Jesus.

13. Any demonic activity affecting my marriage, be terminated, in the name of Jesus.

14. Any program anywhere affecting my marriage, be reduced to right size, in the name of Jesus.

15. Every yoke of immorality upon my marriage, break, in the name of Jesus.

16. O Lord, arise and take over the leadership of my home, in the name of Jesus.

17. Any evil prophecy designed to destroy my marriage, be rejected completely, in the name of Jesus.

18. Every demonic deceit oppressing my marriage, die, in the name of Jesus.

19. Every demonic conspiracy against my marriage, be frustrated, in the name of Jesus.

20. O Lord, help my family to desire spiritual blessings over temporary things, in the name of Jesus.

21. I reject the pursuit of prosperity and abundance without holiness and truth, in the name of Jesus.

22. Let the influence of strange people die in my marriage forever, in the name of Jesus.

23. Let my marriage arise and embrace total deliverance, in the name of Jesus.

1. O Lord, bring back Your mercies into my marriage, in the name of Jesus.

2. Let every unanswered prayers of my marriage be answered, in the name of Jesus.

3. My marriage will not experience mysterious losses, in the name of Jesus.

4. Every arrow of death fired against my marriage, backfire, in the name of Jesus.

5. I reject every demonic dominion over my marriage, in the name of Jesus.

6. Let all the glory of God that departed from my marriage come back double, in the name of Jesus.

7. Every voice of strange man or woman in my marriage, be silenced, in the name of Jesus.

8. My marriage will not forsake divine guide and the vows of marriage, in the name of Jesus.

9. Any other covenant conflicting with the covenant of my marriage, break, in the name of Jesus.

10. Any curse placed upon my marriage by anyone living or dead, expire, in the name of Jesus.

11. O Lord, bring my marriage into the path of life again, in the name of Jesus.

12. Let thorns of cares, riches and pleasures attacking my marriage be roasted by fire, in the name of Jesus.

13. Anything choking the Word of truth in my family, be roasted by fire, in the name of Jesus.

14. Every judgment passed against my marriage, be reversed to my favor, in the name of Jesus.

15. Any serpent in the garden of my marriage, I break your head to pieces, in the name of Jesus.

16. Let the author of sin in my marriage be disgraced by fire, in the name of Jesus.

17. Let the voice of the serpent in the garden of my marriage be disgraced, in the name of Jesus.

18. Every liar in my marriage, be disgraced, in the name of Jesus.

19. I refuse to look at the forbidden fruits in the garden of my marriage, in the name of Jesus.

20. Any power fighting against God's Word in my marriage, die, in the name of Jesus.

21. Blood of Jesus, flow into my marriage and heal every wound, in the name of Jesus.

22. Let the root of sin and problem die in my marriage, in the name of Jesus.

23. O Lord, arise and take my marriage out of every evil prison yard, in the name of Jesus.

1. Father Lord, arise and intervene in my marriage, in the name of Jesus.

2. Any evil personality that has married me or my partner in the spirit, die, in the name of Jesus.

3. I break every evil link between my marriage and any strange person, in the name of Jesus.

4. Let problem arise between my partner and any evil person in my marriage, in the name of Jesus.

5. Anything that is promoting my marriage and any evil partner, die, in the name of Jesus.

6. Every arrow of polygamy in my marriage, I fire you back, in the name of Jesus.

7. O Lord, send confusion into the camp of the enemies of my marriage, in the name of Jesus.

8. I command irreparable division to come between my marriage and its enemies, in the name of Jesus.

9. Any evil personality that has vowed to take over my home, die, in the name of Jesus.

10. Every evil judgment against my marriage, be reversed, in the name of Jesus.

11. Every open door created to bring in strangers into my home, be closed, in the name of Jesus.

12. Every fake lion or lioness in my marriage, die by force, in the name of Jesus.

13. Any demon backing up evil relationships in my marriage, be cast out, in the name of Jesus.

14. Any stranger militating against my marriage, be disgraced, in the name of Jesus.

15. Every evil relationship going on against my marriage, be disconnected, in the name of Jesus.

16. Let confusion swallow every enemy of my marriage by fire, in the name of Jesus.

17. Any stranger sitting upon my marriage, be unseated by death, in the name of Jesus.

18. I command agents of demonic love upon my marriage to die, in the name of Jesus.

19. Let unrepentant agents of darkness troubling my marriage be troubled unto death, in the name of Jesus.

20. Every demonic wound in my marriage, receive divine removal now, in the name of Jesus.

21. Any serpent that has entered in to my marriage, come out and die, in the name of Jesus.

22. I command the enemies of my marriage to vomit every good thing they have swallowed, in the name of Jesus.

23. Lord Jesus, take over my marriage forever, in the name of Jesus.

1. Any evil leg that has walked into my home, walk out by force, in the name of Jesus.

2. Any evil trap set to catch my marriage, catch your owner immediately, in the name of Jesus.

3. Let every serpentine poison in my marriage be neutralized, in the name of Jesus.

4. Any evil association against my marriage, scatter in shame, in the name of Jesus.

5. Every serpentine activity in the garden of my marriage, die, in the name of Jesus.

6. I command every satanic rooted problem in my marriage to be uprooted, in the name of Jesus.

7. Every weapon of destruction in my marriage, catch fire, in the name of Jesus.

8. Let the head of the ancient serpent in my marriage be crushed, in the name of Jesus.

9. O Lord, arise and frustrate household enemies of my marriage, in the name of Jesus.

10. Let the head of Goliath that has risen against my marriage be cut off, in the name of Jesus.

11. Every enemy of my marriage, be exposed unto death, in the name of Jesus.

12. Blood of Jesus, speak my marriage out of destruction, in the name of Jesus.

13. Any grave that has buried my marriage, open and vomit it now, in the name of Jesus.

14. Every injury the enemy has inflicted on my marriage, receive healing, in the name of Jesus.

15. Every enemy troubling my marriage, be wasted, in the name of Jesus.

16. Any evil personality militating against my marriage, be frustrated, in the name of Jesus.

17. Any evil grip on my marriage, lose your hold by fire, in the name of Jesus.

18. I turn the eyes of my partner from strangers in our marriage, in the name of Jesus.

19. I command every marriage breaker in my marriage to die, in the name of Jesus.

20. Every stronghold of the enemy in my marriage, collapse by thunder, in the name of Jesus.

21. Let the backbone of the enemies of my marriage break, in the name of Jesus.

22. Let all supporters of the enemies of my marriage withdraw their supports, in the name of Jesus.

1. I command my marriage to walk out from foundational bondage by fire, in the name of Jesus.

2. Every inherited and personal bondage upon my marriage, break, in the name of Jesus.

3. Let every envious rivalry against my marriage be disgraced, in the name of Jesus.

4. Let the blood of Jesus flush out every problem in my marriage, in the name of Jesus.

5. Every demonic alteration of my marriage destiny, lose your hold over my marriage, in the name of Jesus.

6. I break and loose my marriage from the control of demonic marriage, in the name of Jesus.

7. Every foundational strongman against my marriage, die, in the name of Jesus.

8. Let every gate opened to enemies into my marriage be closed forever, in the name of Jesus.

9. Any demonic sacrifice against my marriage, expire, in the name of Jesus.

10. Any evil and unrepentant diviners against my marriage, die, in the name of Jesus.

11. Any local idol attacking my marriage, be frustrated unto death, in the name of Jesus.

12. Let every inherited family marital pattern of problems die, in the name of Jesus.

13. Any evil plantation against my marriage by the household enemy, die, in the name of Jesus.

14. Any witch or wizard that has bewitched my marriage, be frustrated, in the name of Jesus.

15. Let every secret of the enemies of my marriage be exposed to their shame, in the name of Jesus.

16. O Lord, deliver my marriage from the hand of the wicked, in the name of Jesus.

17. Every evil load upon my marriage, be lifted by force, in the name of Jesus.

18. Every demonic mirror monitoring my marriage, break to pieces, in the name of Jesus.

19. Every evil program designed to overthrow my marriage, turn to my favor, in the name of Jesus.

20. Every satanic influence designed to destroy my marriage, die, in the name of Jesus.

21. Every satanic organized network against my marriage, be disintegrated, in the name of Jesus.

22. Let all hidden enemy of my marriage be exposed unto death, in the name of Jesus.

23. Father Lord, deliver my marriage from determined marriage breakers, in the name of Jesus.

1. Let the fire of God enter into my marriage and burn to ashes every enemy of my destiny, in the name of Jesus.

2. I command every organized strategy of the marriage breakers to fail, in the name of Jesus.

3. Let all executors of conflict and hostility in my marriage be wasted, in the name of Jesus.

4. You my partner sitting on my place in this marriage, be relocated to your place, in the name of Jesus.

5. O Lord, reorder everything in my marriage to glorify Your name, in the name of Jesus.

6. Any satanic designer working against my marriage, be frustrated, in the name of Jesus.

7. Let the brain of the enemy redrawing the map of my marriage scatter, in the name of Jesus.

8. Any evil force that has arrested my marriage, release if by force, in the name of Jesus.

9. Any evil power licking the honey of my marriage, vomit it and die, in the name of Jesus.

10. Any evil counselor against my marriage, be disgraced by confusion, in the name of Jesus.

11. Let the strongman anointed to wreck my marriage die in shame, in the name of Jesus.

12. O Lord, manifest Your power in my marriage by fire, in the name of Jesus.

13. Any evil plan against my marriage, die, in the name of Jesus.

14. Let stubborn enemies of my marriage kill themselves, in the name of Jesus.

15. Let the spirit of hatred attacking my marriage be cast out, in the name of Jesus.

16. I deliver my marriage from the hands of the witches and wizards, in the name of Jesus.

17. Every satanic embargo placed upon my marriage, be lifted, in the name of Jesus.

18. Every internal and external enemy of my marriage, be disgraced, in the name of Jesus.

19. Every wall of difference between me and my partner, collapse, in the name of Jesus.

20. Let the angels of God pursue every enemy of my marriage unto death, in the name of Jesus.

21. Let all evil gang up against my marriage be dispersed, in the name of Jesus.

22. O Lord, force every wicked killer of marriage out of my marriage, in the name of Jesus.

1. Blood of Jesus, close every communication gap between my partner and me, in the name of Jesus.

2. Power to leave and cleave, possess my life partner and me by fire, in the name of Jesus.

3. Let happiness my enemies have stolen from my marriage return double-fold, in the name of Jesus.

4. I command every demonic property in my marriage to be removed forever, in the name of Jesus.

5. I take back by force every place given to devil in my marriage, in the name of Jesus.

6. No gossip, false prophecy or any evil will be allowed to destroy my marriage, in the name of Jesus.

7. Let every demonic suspicion in my marriage be forsaken unto death, in the name of Jesus.

8. Spirit of worldliness and extravagancy in my marriage, be cast out, in the name of Jesus.

9. O Lord, help my marriage to live by divine standards, in the name of Jesus.

10. Any demonic comparison attacking the peace of my marriage, die, in the name of Jesus.

11. Every unforgiving spirit and criticism in my marriage, die, in the name of Jesus.

12. Any power attacking God's love in this marriage, be destroyed by death, in the name of Jesus.

13. O Lord, empower my life partner and me with increased affection, in the name of Jesus.

14. Any demonic affection tearing my marriage apart, die, in the name of Jesus.

15. Any strange man or woman that has vowed to break my marriage, die, in the name of Jesus.

16. I withdraw every negative feeling attacking my marriage, in the name of Jesus.

17. I command impatience, malice, strife, nagging and bitterness to leave my marriage forever, in the name of Jesus.

18. Any evil power displacing marriage positioning in this home, die, in the name of Jesus.

19. Let the spirit of male abdication and female usurpation in this marriage die, in the name of Jesus.

20. Any power assigned to make the man a part-time nurse, maid and baby sitter in this marriage, die, in the name of Jesus.

21. Every yoke of pride, arrogance and powerlessness in this marriage, die forever, in the name of Jesus.

1. Every arrow of spiritual and physical barrenness fired against my life, backfire, in the name of Jesus.

2. Any power assigned to kill my children before birth, die, in the name of Jesus.

3. Any power assigned to kill my children while they are alive, die, in the name of Jesus.

4. Every serpent of polygamy in the garden of my marriage, die, in the name of Jesus.

5. Let powers of wrong marriage that arrested me release me, in the name of Jesus.

6. Any problem that money brought into my marriage, die, in the name of Jesus.

7. Any vacuum my business and other activities have created in my marriage, be filled, in the name of Jesus.

8. O Lord, deliver my marriage from borrowing and begging, in the name of Jesus.

9. Any spirit of debts in my marriage, I cast you out by fire, in the name of Jesus.

10. Every arrow of poverty fired into my marriage, I fire you back, in the name of Jesus.

11. Any agent of separation against my marriage, be disgraced, in the name of Jesus.

12. O Lord, bring me and my partner together, body, soul and spirit, in the name of Jesus.

13. Any serpent of divorce in the garden of my marriage, die, in the name of Jesus.

14. Any power that has vowed to bring divorce and remarriage in this family, die, in the name of Jesus.

15. Holy Ghost fire, burn to ashes every enemy of peace in this marriage, in the name of Jesus.

16. O Lord, make my marriage happy and indissoluble forever, in the name of Jesus.

17. My marital life will not be forced to permissive will, in the name of Jesus.

18. O Lord, empower my marriage to cross every Red Sea, in the name of Jesus.

19. Every enemy of my marriage, be destroyed, in the name of Jesus.

20. O Lord, arise and destroy barrenness in my family forever, in the name of Jesus.

21. Any evil utterance against my marriage, expire, in the name of Jesus.

22. O Lord, help me to move my marriage from every problem, in the name of Jesus.

1. Any satanic priest offering sacrifices against my marriage, be disgraced, in the name of Jesus.

2. Any evil candle burnt against my marriage, backfire, in the name of Jesus.

3. Blood of Jesus, deliver my marriage from every evil offering, in the name of Jesus.

4. Let my marriage escape from every evil altar, in the name of Jesus.

5. Let my marriage receive every good thing it has lost to the devil, in the name of Jesus.

6. Any evil kingdom attacking my marriage, scatter in shame, in the name of Jesus.

7. I release my marriage from unprofitable friendships, in the name of Jesus.

8. Any dark power manipulating my marriage, be manipulated, in the name of Jesus.

9. Every demonic authority assigned to waste my marriage, be disgraced, in the name of Jesus.

10. Let every evil remote controller against my marriage lose its hold, in the name of Jesus.

11. I release my marriage from hold of every witchcraft attacks, in the name of Jesus.

12. Blood of Jesus, deliver my marriage from every strange authority, in the name of Jesus.

13. I break and loose my life partner and I from evil soul ties, in the name of Jesus.

14. Every desire and expectation of enemies of my marriage, die, in the name of Jesus.

15. Every ungodly relationship against my marriage, break, in the name of Jesus.

16. Every evil soul-tie with any adulterer, break by force, in the name of Jesus.

17. Any close friend hunting for my marriage, be disgraced, in the name of Jesus.

18. Any evil organization attacking my marriage, scatter, in the name of Jesus.

19. Let all my past and present evil friends against my marriage be disgraced, in the name of Jesus.

20. Any power assigned to subject my marriage to evil attacks, die, in the name of Jesus.

21. Any evil affection assigned to destroy my marriage, die, in the name of Jesus.

22. I reject every evil advanced to waste my marriage, in the name of Jesus.

23. Let our Lord Jesus capture and control my affection and emotions forever, in the name of Jesus.

Day 12

1. Any dark power manipulating marriage in my environment, I am not your candidate, in the name of Jesus.

2. Let the divine purpose for my marriage begin to manifest, in the name of Jesus.

3. Let divine plan for my marital fulfillment begin to manifest, in the name of Jesus.

4. Any negative action taken against my marriage, be destroyed, in the name of Jesus.

5. Anything that needs to be uprooted out of my marriage, be uprooted, in the name of Jesus.

6. Any wound and injury done to my marriage, be healed, in the name of Jesus.

7. Any strongman that is fighting my marriage, be destroyed, in the name of Jesus.

8. Let every good plan for my marriage begin to manifest, in the name of Jesus.

9. Every spirit of misunderstanding in my home, be destroyed, in the name of Jesus.

10. Every wicked device against my marriage, backfire, in the name of Jesus.

11. Every instrument of marriage destroyers in my life, catch fire, in the name of Jesus.

12. Any evil thing the enemy has invested in my marriage, receive fire, in the name of Jesus.

13. Any spirit man or woman that has married anyone in my family, die, in the name of Jesus.

14. I break and loose everyone in my family from any evil relationship, in the name of Jesus.

15. Any evil force that is sponsoring my marital problems, scatter in shame, in the name of Jesus.

16. I break and loose my marriage from every evil marriage link, in the name of Jesus.

17. Any evil personality interfering in my marriage, die by fire, in the name of Jesus.

18. Any aborted blood crying against my marriage, be silenced by Jesus, in the name of Jesus.

19. Every wrong done against my marriage, be corrected by fire, in the name of Jesus.

20. Every evil imagination, thoughts, desires and expectations against my marriage, die, in the name of Jesus.

21. Any power that has vowed to put my marriage asunder, be disgraced, in the name of Jesus.

22. Father Lord, empower my marriage to stand, in the name of Jesus.

Day 13

1. Every spiritual evil relationship attacking my marriage, be disgraced, in the name of Jesus.

2. Every conscious and unconscious covenant working against my marriage, expire, in the name of Jesus.

3. Any spirit of worldliness and extravagance in my marriage, be cast out, in the name of Jesus.

4. I command every domineering character working against my marriage to die, in the name of Jesus.

5. O Lord, deliver my marriage from demonic and poor communication, in the name of Jesus.

6. Let the spirit of worry and criticism be cast out of my marriage, in the name of Jesus.

7. Any spirit of hatred, anger and selfishness, be cast out of my marriage, in the name of Jesus.

8. O Lord, help me to know how to approach every problem in my marriage with understanding, in the name of Jesus.

9. I command every spirit of bad leadership example in my marriage to die, in the name of Jesus.

10. Let every spirit of sin and backslide leave my marriage forever, in the name of Jesus.

11. O Lord, teach me how to speak boldly in my family, in the name of Jesus.

12. Every spirit of hardship, harsh word, lying and infirmity in my marriage, die, in the name of Jesus.

13. Any evil power that has vowed to break my home, fail woefully, in the name of Jesus.

14. I bind and cast out every spirit husband and wife in my marriage, in the name of Jesus.

15. Any property of the dark kingdom in my home, I remove you forever, in the name of Jesus.

16. Let evil powers that wreck homes fail woefully in my marriage, in the name of Jesus.

17. Lion of Judah, enter into my marriage and drive away every fake lion, in the name of Jesus.

18. Father Lord, transform my marriage to your original plan and purpose, in the name of Jesus.

19. I command my marriage to be anointed to prosper all round, in the name of Jesus.

20. Any evil personality hired to destroy my marriage, destroy yourself and your sender, in the name of Jesus.

21. Any evil altar that has arrested the eagle of my marriage, release it, in the name of Jesus.

22. Every evil counsel against my marriage, die, in the name of Jesus.

23. Holy Ghost fire, burn to ashes every enemy of my marriage, in the name of Jesus.

1. Blood of Jesus, remove every demonic weakness in my marriage, in the name of Jesus.

2. Every good dream ever dreamt about my marriage, begin to manifest, in the name of Jesus.

3. Let the hand of evil designers upon my marriage wither, in the name of Jesus.

4. Any satanic vehicle driving my marriage to wrong places, scatter, in the name of Jesus.

5. Every stronghold built in the waters against my marriage, collapse, in the name of Jesus.

6. O Lord, readjust my marriage to bear fruit and be fulfilled, in the name of Jesus.

7. O Lord, establish divine character in my home and bless my marriage, in the name of Jesus.

8. Let the map of my marriage remain as God has drawn it, in the name of Jesus.

9. Every property of the queen of heaven in my marriage, be roasted by fire, in the name of Jesus.

10. Any evil partner that has replaced divine partners in my family, be removed, in the name of Jesus.

11. Every seed of failure planted into my marriage, die immediately, in the name of Jesus.

12. Every good thing the enemy has removed from my marriage, come back, in the name of Jesus.

13. Any attack in my marriage from my place of birth, be terminated, in the name of Jesus.

14. I close the mouth of everyone that is speaking against my marriage, in the name of Jesus.

15. Let the spirit of sex outside marriage threatening my marriage, be cast out, in the name of Jesus.

16. Every demon of rigidity, intolerance and accusation in my marriage, die, in the name of Jesus.

17. Let the powers of laziness, lack of appreciation and stubbornness depart from my home, in the name of Jesus.

18. Let the divine wall of defense surround my home to keep my marriage, in the name of Jesus.

19. Any spirit of conflict and hostility frustrating my marriage, be cast out, in the name of Jesus.

20. I cast out every spirit of ego, self-centeredness and negative emotions from my marriage, in the name of Jesus.

21. Blood of Jesus, provoke my marriage to divine love, in the name of Jesus.

22. Let my life move towards the right direction from henceforth, in the name of Jesus.

1. Every yoke of evil association upon my marriage, break to pieces, in the name of Jesus.

2. I detached my marriage from evil attachments with our parents, in the name of Jesus.

3. Any of our parents that have refused to leave my marriage alone, be convicted by the Holy Spirit, in the name of Jesus.

4. Any polluted wind directed against my marriage, go back to your sender, in the name of Jesus.

5. Any evil river flowing into my marriage, dry up immediately, in the name of Jesus.

6. Any witchcraft power that wastes marriage, my marriage is not for you, in the name of Jesus.

7. Let every sexual demon in my marriage be arrested unto death, in the name of Jesus.

8. Let the knowledge of God's Word come upon my marriage, in the name of Jesus.

9. I cast out of my marriage the spirit of selfishness, in the name of Jesus.

10. Let every unsaved person in my family be saved by divine mercy, in the name of Jesus.

11. Every foolish action motivated to destroy my marriage, fail woefully, in the name of Jesus.

12. O Lord, deliver my marriage from collapse as result of carelessness, in the name of Jesus.

13. O Lord, empower my family altar to recover all that my marriage has lost, in the name of Jesus.

14. I reject every unprofitable imitation and comparison against my family, in the name of Jesus.

15. I command any relationship that is designed to destroy my marriage to die, in the name of Jesus.

16. O Lord, give me financial breakthrough that will deliver my marriage, in the name of Jesus.

17. I command my marriage to receive the power to produce godly children, in the name of Jesus.

18. Let divine respect for God and family members prevail in my family, in the name of Jesus.

19. I command everything that will make my family happy to manifest, in the name of Jesus.

20. Let my marriage be a good example to other marriages, in the name of Jesus.

21. Everyone that is possessed in my family, receive full deliverance, in the name of Jesus.

22. My children will not be a reproach, in the name of Jesus.

Day 16

1. I release my marriage from demonic arrest of spirit of death, in the name of Jesus.

2. Every area of my marriage that is dead, come alive by force, in the name of Jesus.

3. Every wounded part of my marriage, receive divine healing, in the name of Jesus.

4. O Lord, command Your breath of life to enter into my marriage now, in the name of Jesus.

5. Every evil force assigned to kill my marriage, scatter and die, in the name of Jesus.

6. Let all marriage killers about to kill my marriage be paralyzed, in the name of Jesus.

7. Every arrow of household enemy against my marriage, backfire, in the name of Jesus.

8. I command my partner to be tired of cooperating with enemies of our marriage, in the name of Jesus.

9. Any power that wants to put my marriage to an end, be disgraced, in the name of Jesus.

10. Any unfriendly friend attacking my marriage, be exposed and disgraced, in the name of Jesus.

11. I command the glory of God that left my marriage to return by God's mercy, in the name of Jesus.

12. Blood of Jesus, prosper my marriage and move it forward, in the name of Jesus.

13. Let every seed of witchcraft planted in my marriage die, in the name of Jesus.

14. I command my marriage to leave every evil altar that captured it, in the name of Jesus.

15. Every agent of home breaking, be frustrated with shame, in the name of Jesus.

16. Any power sponsoring enemies of my marriage, be wasted, in the name of Jesus.

17. Any witchcraft dog barking against my marriage, be silenced unto death, in the name of Jesus.

18. I deliver my marriage from afflictions, in the name of Jesus.

19. Any false allegation against my marriage, be terminated to my favor, in the name of Jesus.

20. Any evil power sitting upon my marital promotion, be unseated by death, in the name of Jesus.

21. Any power attacking the star of my marriage, be disgraced, in the name of Jesus.

22. Any fainting spirit that is attacking the strength of my marriage, die, in the name of Jesus.

23. Any bewitchment fashioned against my marriage, be destroyed, in the name of Jesus.

1. Every instrument of bewitchment against my marriage, be rendered impotent, in the name of Jesus.

2. Every untamed enemy of my marriage, be tamed by fire, in the name of Jesus.

3. O Lord, release Your angels to intervene in my marriage, in the name of Jesus.

4. Every satanic program going on against my marriage, be terminated, in the name of Jesus.

5. Every battle going on in the waters against my marriage, end to my favor, in the name of Jesus.

6. Every satanic debt collector working against my marriage, die, in the name of Jesus.

7. Let the blood of Jesus speak my marriage out of every debt, in the name of Jesus.

8. Any evil personality attacking my marriage from the heavenlies, die, in the name of Jesus.

9. Let every evil mark upon my marriage be roasted by fire, in the name of Jesus.

10. I release divine military angels to fight until my marriage is set free, in the name of Jesus.

11. Every enemy of my marital freedom, die, in the name of Jesus.

12. Ancient of days deliver my marriage from ancestral captivity, in the name of Jesus.

13. Let the oppressors of my marriage begin to oppress themselves, in the name of Jesus.

14. Let angels of the living God trample upon enemies of my marriage, in the name of Jesus.

15. Let all evil speakers against my marriage become dumb forever, in the name of Jesus.

16. Any evil decree passed against my marriage, be revoked by force, in the name of Jesus.

17. Let my prayers become too hot against the enemies of my marriage, in the name of Jesus.

18. O God, arise and anoint my marriage to receive power to fulfill its call, in the name of Jesus.

19. Let the backbone of the enemies of my marriage break to pieces, in the name of Jesus.

20. I release my marriage from bondage of known and unknown curses, in the name of Jesus.

21. Let the devourers of my marriage be devoured unto death, in the name of Jesus.

22. Let the workers of iniquity against my marriage be wasted, in the name of Jesus.

23. Any satanic chain holding my marriage in hostage, break, in the name of Jesus.

1. Anything representing my marriage in altars of death, burn to ashes, in the name of Jesus.

2. O Lord, deliver my marriage from any evil judgment passed against it, in the name of Jesus.

3. Let the desires of the wicked over my marriage be frustrated, in the name of Jesus.

4. Any power that wants my marriage to miscarry her blessings, die, in the name of Jesus.

5. O Lord, arise and take my marriage to victory, in the name of Jesus.

6. My marriage will not be converted to living dead, in the name of Jesus.

7. Any dry bone of my marriage, arise and receive resurrection, in the name of Jesus.

8. Let every coffin prepared to bury my marriage be roasted by fire, in the name of Jesus.

9. Every satanic full stop in my marriage, disappear, in the name of Jesus.

10. You my marriage, move forward by force, in the name of Jesus.

11. Any evil decision taken anywhere against my marriage, be reversed, in the name of Jesus.

12. Any evil consultation going on against my marriage, scatter, in the name of Jesus.

13. Any evil cloud gathering against my marriage, scatter, in the name of Jesus.

14. Let the wind of Judgment carry away every marital problem in my home, in the name of Jesus.

15. Every internal disorder against my marriage, receive divine order, in the name of Jesus.

16. Let every hidden problem in my marriage be exposed and disgraced, in the name of Jesus.

17. Every architect of marital crisis, die, in the name of Jesus.

18. Holy Ghost, empower me to be an instrument You will use to deliver many marriages, in the name of Jesus.

19. Any evil power that wants to harvest my marriage, die in shame, in the name of Jesus.

20. I command every evil presence in my marriage to disappear by force, in the name of Jesus.

21. Blood of Jesus, empower me to celebrate the fulfillment of my marriage vow, in the name of Jesus.

22. I reject every spirit of separation and divorce, in the name of Jesus.

23. Let every problem in my marriage receive immediate destruction, in the name of Jesus.

1. Every evil yoke linking my marriage to marital unrest, break, in the name of Jesus.

2. Every spirit of crisis in my marriage, be frustrated, in the name of Jesus.

3. Let all curses and evil covenants speaking against my marriage be destroyed, in the name of Jesus.

4. O Lord, empower me to enjoy my marriage as You have ordained, in the name of Jesus.

5. Every evil pattern of marital problem in my life, be disorganized, in the name of Jesus.

6. Every agent of marital failure in my life, be frustrated, in the name of Jesus.

7. O Lord, connect my marriage to all her helpers, in the name of Jesus.

8. Father Lord, help me to discover real joy and peace in my marriage, in the name of Jesus.

9. Let every evil imagination of enemies against my marriage be rendered null and void, in the name of Jesus.

10. Every evil agreement against my marriage, be rendered impotent, in the name of Jesus.

11. Every covenant of marital failure in my marriage, break, in the name of Jesus.

12. Every generational curse against my marriage, be revoked in my marriage, in the name of Jesus.

13. O Lord, arise and bless my marriage with all manner of blessings, in the name of Jesus.

14. Any yoke of hardship against my marriage, break to pieces, in the name of Jesus.

15. Any power working against my marriage, break to pieces, in the name of Jesus.

16. Every covenant I entered into that is now affecting my marriage, break, in the name of Jesus.

17. Every poison invested in my marriage, lose your power, in the name of Jesus.

18. Any evil covenant my partner entered into that is now affecting my marriage, break, in the name of Jesus.

19. Any evil pot cooking my marriage into trouble, break to pieces, in the name of Jesus.

20. Holy spirit, overhaul my marriage and cleanse it from corruption, in the name of Jesus.

21. Any marine spirit cauldron cooking my marriage, catch fire and break, in the name of Jesus.

22. Anointing for supernatural peace, fall upon my marriage, in the name of Jesus.

23. Any foreign hand attacking my marriage, dry up by fire, in the name of Jesus.

1. O Lord, deliver my marriage from consequences of all past sexual sins, in the name of Jesus.

2. Let every attack coming from the waters against my marriage cease, in the name of Jesus.

3. Any evil gift I received that is affecting my marriage, be destroyed, in the name of Jesus.

4. Any demonic attachment to my marriage, catch fire, in the name of Jesus.

5. O Lord, reactivate my marriage and push it forward, in the name of Jesus.

6. Father Lord, renew Your commitment to bless my marriage, in the name of Jesus.

7. Every hidden darkness that captured my marriage, release it by force, in the name of Jesus.

8. Every evil presence residing in my home, I cast you out, in the name of Jesus.

9. Every hidden enemy of my marriage, be exposed unto death, in the name of Jesus.

10. Every deadly weapon prepared against my marriage, catch fire, in the name of Jesus.

11. Any dark spirit moving around my home, be disgraced forever, in the name of Jesus.

12. Any power that has stolen peace and joy from my marriage, return it and die, in the name of Jesus.

13. I disconnect my marriage from every evil contact known and unknown, in the name of Jesus.

14. Any evil record affecting my marriage, be erased by the blood of Jesus, in the name of Jesus.

15. Every abnormal movement against my marriage, cease by force and die, in the name of Jesus.

16. Any power sponsoring problems in my marriage, be disgraced publicly, in the name of Jesus.

17. I command all long term bondages in my marriage to break by force, in the name of Jesus.

18. Any evil altar harboring problems against my marriage, be roasted by fire, in the name of Jesus.

19. Every evil decision taking against my marriage, be reversed, in the name of Jesus.

20. Every spiritual weapon fashioned against my marriage, backfire, in the name of Jesus.

21. Every satanic influence on my marriage, be disorganized, in the name of Jesus.

22. Blood of Jesus, restore and reconcile my marriage with all good blessings, in the name of Jesus.

Day 21

1. Every arrow of backwardness fired at my marriage, backfire, in the name of Jesus.

2. Any power pulling my marriage down, I cut off your existence, in the name of Jesus.

3. Any evil structure constructed against my marriage spiritually or physically, be uprooted, in the name of Jesus.

4. You that power that has vowed to convert my home to a war zone, die, in the name of Jesus.

5. Thou sword of deliverance, deliver my marriage from every trouble, in the name of Jesus.

6. O Lord, arise and gather all fragmented parts of my marriage together, in the name of Jesus.

7. Any spirit of tail attacking my marriage, I cut you off, in the name of Jesus.

8. Let every witchcraft garment upon my marriage catch fire, in the name of Jesus.

9. Anointing to move forward, fall upon my marriage, in the name of Jesus.

10. Father Lord, manifest Your glory in my marriage, in the name of Jesus.

11. Any power that is scattering my marriage, surrender, bow and die, in the name of Jesus.

12. Every unconscious or conscious handover of my marriage to the kingdom of darkness, be revoked, in the name of Jesus.

13. O Lord, arise and command Your wind to gather my marriage together, in the name of Jesus.

14. Any satanic bird or fowl released against my marriage, die, in the name of Jesus.

15. Any enemy that I mistakenly brought into my marriage, be disgraced out, in the name of Jesus.

16. Father Lord, arise and rearrange my marriage again by Your power, in the name of Jesus.

17. O Lord, command Your anointing and favor to fall upon my marriage, in the name of Jesus.

18. Father Lord, label my marriage with Your divine favor, in the name of Jesus.

19. Any burial procession organized against my marriage, be disbanded, in the name of Jesus.

20. Any witchcraft broom sweeping away my marriage, be roasted by fire, in the name of Jesus.

21. Any cobweb mounted against my marriage, catch fire, in the name of Jesus.

22. Every shame, disgrace and reproach against my marriage, be destroyed, in the name of Jesus.

23. Let God arise and overthrow every enemy of my marriage, in the name of Jesus.

1. Any foundational witchcraft embargo placed upon my marriage, be lifted, in the name of Jesus.

2. Let every family altar crying against my marriage be scattered by fire, in the name of Jesus.

3. Any evil priest or wicked personality ministering against my marriage, die, in the name of Jesus.

4. Let the idol that is against my marriage be uprooted by fire, in the name of Jesus.

5. Any weakness and defects affecting my marriage, be destroyed by fire, in the name of Jesus.

6. You the darkness covering the glory of my marriage, disappear by force, in the name of Jesus.

7. Every covenant of failure upon my marriage, be broken, in the name of Jesus.

8. Any evil character tearing my marriage apart, die, in the name of Jesus.

9. Let the cry of any evil altar against my marriage be silenced, in the name of Jesus.

10. I reject every family carryover of evil into my marriage, in the name of Jesus.

11. Any satanic barriers against my marriage, be removed by force, in the name of Jesus.

12. Any evil dedication affecting my marriage, be revoked by force, in the name of Jesus.

13. Every architect of problems in my marriage, receive destruction, in the name of Jesus.

14. Every spiritual wolf against my marriage, be paralyzed, in the name of Jesus.

15. Every curse of automatic failure in my marriage, break, in the name of Jesus.

16. Any wicked man or woman that vowed to destroy my marriage, destroy yourself, in the name of Jesus.

17. Every demon of sexual perversion that entered into my marriage, die, in the name of Jesus.

18. Every past sexual sin holding my marriage in bondage, drink the blood of Jesus, in the name of Jesus.

19. I set ablaze every witchcraft altar militating against my marriage, in the name of Jesus.

20. Any power from the waters promoting conflicts and hostilities in my home, die, in the name of Jesus.

21. Let all spiritual armed robbers against my marriage be wasted, in the name of Jesus.

22. Every satanic activity against my marriage in the dream, be terminated, in the name of Jesus.

23. I deliver my marriage from the hands of evil designers, in the name of Jesus.

1. You the disorganized map of my marriage, be arranged together again, in the name of Jesus.

2. Every satanic influence over my marriage, be canceled by the blood of Jesus, in the name of Jesus.

3. I command my marriage to escape from the hands of marriage manipulating experts, in the name of Jesus.

4. Every decision taken against my marriage at any witchcraft gathering, be nullified, in the name of Jesus.

5. I command every garment of marital break-up to catch fire in my marriage, in the name of Jesus.

6. Every anti-marriage forces working hard to destroy my marriage, scatter, in the name of Jesus.

7. Blood of Jesus, return every spiritual dowry and other things working against my marriage, in the name of Jesus.

8. Let the presence of God return fully in my marriage, in the name of Jesus.

9. Let the cause of every problem in my marriage be traced and destroyed, in the name of Jesus.

10. Every property or link with spirit wife or husband in my marriage, catch fire, in the name of Jesus.

11. Every strange fire burning in my marriage, be quenched by force, in the name of Jesus.

12. I command the heavens of my marriage to break open, in the name of Jesus.

13. Every home wrecker attacking my marriage, be frustrated, in the name of Jesus.

14. Any vow in the spirit to break my marriage, be broken by, in the name of Jesus.

15. Every evil counsel by suicide mission demon against my marriage, fail, in the name of Jesus.

16. Every determined enemy of my marriage, scatter and die in shame, in the name of Jesus.

17. Any evil personality with unrepentant and uncompromising vow to destroy any marriage, die without mercy, in the name of Jesus.

18. I halt every evil movement toward my marriage and declare my marriage untouchable, in the name of Jesus.

19. Any power activating dead problems in my marriage, be destroyed, in the name of Jesus.

20. Let my marriage receive complete freedom from the queen of heaven, in the name of Jesus.

21. Any power leading my marriage to doom, I behead you by force, in the name of Jesus.

22. O Lord, visit my marriage with peace and joy, in the name of Jesus.

23. Every good thing that my marriage has ever lost, come back double, in the name of Jesus.

1. Every yoke of iniquity deeply rooted in my marriage, break, in the name of Jesus.

2. Let the stronghold of iniquity holding my marriage break, in the name of Jesus.

3. Every backbone of sin in my marriage, break to pieces, in the name of Jesus.

4. I command every seed of sin in my marriage to die suddenly, in the name of Jesus.

5. Blood of Jesus, Holy Ghost fire, penetrate into the root of my marriage, in the name of Jesus.

6. Any seed of sin planted in my marriage, be dismantled, in the name of Jesus.

7. I commend my marriage to receive spiritual cleansing by fire, in the name of Jesus.

8. I deliver my marriage from ancestral demonic pollutions, in the name of Jesus.

9. Every throne of iniquity reigning over my marriage, be dethroned, in the name of Jesus.

10. Every generational curse affecting my marriage, expire, in the name of Jesus.

11. I command the root of my marriage to be cleansed by the blood of Jesus, in the name of Jesus.

12. Any evil personality mandated to destroy my marriage, destroy yourself, in the name of Jesus.

13. Any power attacking my marriage from the heavenlies, attack yourself, in the name of Jesus.

14. I command every spirit of death upon my marriage to depart forever, in the name of Jesus.

15. Every bad habit militating against my marriage, die, in the name of Jesus.

16. I command my marriage to follow the path of righteousness, in the name of Jesus.

17. Any evil power that has poisoned my character against my marriage, die, in the name of Jesus.

18. Let the spirit of destruction released into my marriage be cast out, in the name of Jesus.

19. I command the spirit of the beast in my marriage to be disgraced out, in the name of Jesus.

20. Any witch or wizard working round the clock to waste my marriage, be wasted, in the name of Jesus.

21. Let the chains of witchcraft powers against my marriage break, in the name of Jesus.

22. Owners of evil load in my life, appear and carry your load, in the name of Jesus.

23. Any witchcraft powerhouse against my marriage, catch fire, in the name of Jesus.

1. Let the ministry of witchcraft against my marriage be frustrated, in the name of Jesus.

2. Any witchcraft animal programmed into my marriage, come out and die, in the name of Jesus.

3. Let every witchcraft voice against my marriage be silenced, in the name of Jesus.

4. Any strange fire burning my marriage, be quenched by the blood of Jesus, in the name of Jesus.

5. Any evil movement on the sea against my marriage, be demolished, in the name of Jesus.

6. Every force that has dominated my marriage, be paralyzed, in the name of Jesus.

7. I withdraw my marriage from the list of the witchcraft books, in the name of Jesus.

8. Any evil agenda against my marriage, be frustrated by fire, in the name of Jesus.

9. Let the brains of unrepentant witches and wizards against my marriage be roasted by fire, in the name of Jesus.

10. I withdraw my money from the throne of witchcraft powers, in the name of Jesus.

11. Any inherited poverty against my marriage, expire, in the name of Jesus.

12. Any evil force that has enslaved my marriage, release it now, in the name of Jesus.

13. Any witchcraft meeting against my marriage, scatter in shame, in the name of Jesus.

14. Any evil decision taken against my marriage, be frustrated, in the name of Jesus.

15. Any evil flow into my marriage, be terminated by fire, in the name of Jesus.

16. I break to pieces any witchcraft padlock against my marriage, in the name of Jesus.

17. I command every problem that is in the foundation of my marriage to die, in the name of Jesus.

18. Blood of Jesus, repair any damage devil has done against my marriage, in the name of Jesus.

19. Let the blood of Jesus purge my marriage and cleanse it of every impurity, in the name of Jesus.

20. Every evil pronouncement ever uttered against my marriage, be nullified, in the name of Jesus.

21. Any power that does not want my marriage to move forward, be disgraced, in the name of Jesus.

22. Any environmental destroyer of marriages, be destroyed completely, in the name of Jesus.

1. Father Lord, withdraw Your support and strength from the enemies of my marriage, in the name of Jesus.

2. Let original divine design for my marriage manifest, in the name of Jesus.

3. My marriage will not live below divine standard, in the name of Jesus.

4. Every negative statement ever issued against my marriage, expire, in the name of Jesus.

5. Let polluters of my marriage be frustrated by fire, in the name of Jesus.

6. Every damage done against the original copy of my marriage, be repaired, in the name of Jesus.

7. Every demotion targeted against my marriage, be frustrated by fire, in the name of Jesus.

8. Any evil power wasting my marriage, be wasted, in the name of Jesus.

9. Any power that wants to convert my marriage to evil camp, die, in the name of Jesus.

10. Every demonic effort to waste my marriage, be wasted, in the name of Jesus.

11. O Lord, fill my marriage with Spirit of excellence, in the name of Jesus.

12. Any power contending with peace in my marriage, be destroyed, in the name of Jesus.

13. O Lord, enlarge the coast of my marriage, in the name of Jesus.

14. Any evil power bringing problems into my marriage, be disgraced, in the name of Jesus.

15. Let the spirit of death be cast out of my marriage forever, in the name of Jesus.

16. Any area of my marriage occupied by darkness, receive light, in the name of Jesus.

17. Every progress enemies have made over my marriage, I take you away, in the name of Jesus.

18. Every satanic door into my marriage, be closed forever, in the name of Jesus.

19. Every satanic opportunity to destroy my marriage, be frustrated, in the name of Jesus.

20. Any evil power fighting hard to take over my marriage, be disappointed, in the name of Jesus.

21. Let God arise and force the enemies out of my marriage, in the name of Jesus.

22. You my marriage, receive deliverance, in the name of Jesus.

1. Anything planted in my marriage by the enemy, die immediately, in the name of Jesus.

2. Every internal war going on against my marriage, end to my favor, in the name of Jesus.

3. Let the strongman of my marriage die by fire, in the name of Jesus.

4. Let the air suffocate the enemies of my marriage, in the name of Jesus.

5. Any power that wants to take God's place in my marriage, die, in the name of Jesus.

6. Any voice of death released against my marriage, backfire, in the name of Jesus.

7. Let the forces of destruction against my marriage scatter in shame, in the name of Jesus.

8. Any evil assignment to steal peace from my marriage, fail, in the name of Jesus.

9. Every ritual or incantation against my marriage, be frustrated, in the name of Jesus.

10. Let the rod of the water spirits against my marriage rest upon their kingdom, in the name of Jesus.

11. O Lord, bring my marriage back to Your original agenda, in the name of Jesus.

12. I return my marriage back to divine purpose and agenda, in the name of Jesus.

13. Any evil sacrifice offered against my marriage, be destroyed, in the name of Jesus.

14. Every weapon of night raiders against my marriage, be destroyed, in the name of Jesus.

15. Every garment of shame and poverty upon my marriage, burn to ashes, in the name of Jesus.

16. Let every rain of affliction upon my marriage cease by force, in the name of Jesus.

17. Any evil eyes observing my marriage, close forever, in the name of Jesus.

18. Any power prolonging my marriage deliverance, be disgraced, in the name of Jesus.

19. Any progress devil has made over my marriage, I withdraw you now, in the name of Jesus.

20. Let all marriage killer demons upon my marriage be arrested unto death, in the name of Jesus.

21. Any power that has hijacked my marriage, release it and die, in the name of Jesus.

22. Any evil manipulation going on against my marriage, I stop you by force, in the name of Jesus.

1. Any multiple covenant keeping my marriage in bondage, break, in the name of Jesus.

2. Every iron-like curse against my marriage, expire, in the name of Jesus.

3. Let every witchcraft handwriting against my marriage be cleansed, in the name of Jesus.

4. I command all evil bullets fired into my marriage to backfire, in the name of Jesus.

5. Any evil report against my marriage, be converted to my favor, in the name of Jesus.

6. Let the marks of the devil upon my marriage be roasted by fire, in the name of Jesus.

7. Let tragedies designed against my marriage, fail woefully, in the name of Jesus.

8. Any power attacking my marriage from the forest, be disgraced, in the name of Jesus.

9. Any satanic minister ministering against my marriage, die by fire, in the name of Jesus.

10. I command my marriage to come out from every evil coffin, in the name of Jesus.

11. Any vagabond spirit upon my marriage, be frustrated, in the name of Jesus.

12. Any counterfeit blessing upon my marriage, be removed, in the name of Jesus.

13. Any evil fowl of sacrifice against my marriage, die, in the name of Jesus.

14. Blood of Jesus, speak my marriage out of every evil sacrifice, in the name of Jesus.

15. Let the destroying flood of God destroy every problem in my marriage, in the name of Jesus.

16. I command all waters of affliction in my marriage to dry up, in the name of Jesus.

17. Let the anger of the Lord depart from my marriage by God's mercy, in the name of Jesus.

18. Let every enemy of my marriage receive shock by fire, in the name of Jesus.

19. Fire of God, burn to ashes every enemy of my marriage, in the name of Jesus.

20. Let the rage of the devil against my marriage be removed, in the name of Jesus.

21. Any personal stronghold built against my marriage, collapse, in the name of Jesus.

1. Any satanic deposit troubling my marriage, catch fire and burn to ashes, in the name of Jesus.

2. Let every marriage killer demon upon my marriage be disgraced, in the name of Jesus.

3. Any satanic prayers going on against my marriage, expire and backfire, in the name of Jesus.

4. Every evil advertisement against my marriage, be terminated, in the name of Jesus.

5. Every household arrow fired at my marriage, backfire, in the name of Jesus.

6. Every evil reinforcement against my marriage, be frustrated, in the name of Jesus.

7. Any power that has caged my marriage, be frustrate and bow, in the name of Jesus.

8. Any personal territorial strongman against my marriage, die, in the name of Jesus.

9. Any hidden enemy of my marriage, be exposed and disgraced, in the name of Jesus.

10. Any unprofitable load upon my marriage, drop by force, in the name of Jesus.

11. Let every occult arrow fired against my marriage backfire, in the name of Jesus.

12. Let every program of the wicked against my marriage come to an end, in the name of Jesus.

13. Any dream manipulator manipulating my marriage, be disgraced, in the name of Jesus.

14. Let all satanic angels fighting against my marriage be frustrated, in the name of Jesus.

15. O Lord, deliver my marriage from late progress, in the name of Jesus.

16. Every evil prophesy designed to kill my marriage, fail woefully, in the name of Jesus.

17. I command all the shame distributors in my marriages to avoid my marriage, in the name of Jesus.

18. Every evil gate built against my marriage, collapse by thunder, in the name of Jesus.

19. Let the cloud of sorrow in my marriage be dispersed by thunder, in the name of Jesus.

20. Let the whirlwind of God carry away every enemy of my marriage, in the name of Jesus.

21. Any demon on suicide mission against my marriage, die alone, in the name of Jesus.

22. Any satanic agent assigned to destroy my marriage, be destroyed, in the name of Jesus.

23. Let the earth, sea and air quake to release my marriage, in the name of Jesus.

1. Any satanic worm eating up my marriage, die by fire, in the name of Jesus.

2. Every voice of confusion speaking against my marriage, be silenced, in the name of Jesus.

3. Every enemy of my marriage, receive self-destruction, in the name of Jesus.

4. Any disappointment about to take place in my marriage, die, in the name of Jesus.

5. Let the oppressors of my marriage receive double destruction, in the name of Jesus.

6. Let the strongman against my marriage begin to experience failures, in the name of Jesus.

7. Any stubborn problem upon my marriage, die immediately, in the name of Jesus.

8. Any unprofitable love charged with destroying my marriage, die, in the name of Jesus.

9. The progress my marriage has made shall not be destroyed by the enemies, in the name of Jesus.

10. Let the scarcity devil caused in my marriage die, in the name of Jesus.

11. O Lord, bless my marriage with material wealth, in the name of Jesus.

12. Any evil sword enemies have raised against my marriage, drop, in the name of Jesus.

13. Every satanic siren scaring good things out of my marriage, be silenced, in the name of Jesus.

14. Every anti progress spirit against my marriage, die, in the name of Jesus.

15. My marriage shall not crash but prosper, in the name of Jesus.

16. I command the eagle of my marriage to fly to the mountaintop, in the name of Jesus.

17. Any evil gathering because of my marriage, die, in the name of Jesus.

18. Every power working against my marriage, be dismantled, in the name of Jesus.

19. Any door of my marriage blessing locked up by the enemy, open by force, in the name of Jesus.

20. Any power organized to pull me down, be disgraced, in the name of Jesus.

21. My marriage will not accept failure, in the name of Jesus.

22. Every satanic network against my marriage, be frustrated, in the name of Jesus.

23. Let the enemies of my marriage begin to misunderstand themselves, in the name of Jesus.

24. My marriage will not accept evil limitations, in the name of Jesus.

1. Let the head of my marriage's oppressors be crushed, in the name of Jesus.

2. Any satanic attack on the star of my marriage, be frustrated, in the name of Jesus.

3. Any battle fashioned against my marriage, be diverted, in the name of Jesus.

4. Let my marriage be anchored to the Word of God, in the name of Jesus.

5. Any power assigned to frustrate my marriage, be frustrated, in the name of Jesus.

6. Let peace of God reign supreme in my marriage, in the name of Jesus.

7. Let weapons of strange man or woman against my marriage backfire, in the name of Jesus.

8. O Lord, arise and be the redeemer of my marriage, in the name of Jesus.

9. Every hindrance on my way to marriage prosperity, be removed, in the name of Jesus.

10. Every satanic blockage against my marriage, be removed, in the name of Jesus.

11. I deliver my marriage from every evil inheritance, in the name of Jesus.

12. Let powers of unrepentant household wickedness against my marriage fail, in the name of Jesus.

13. O Lord, anoint my marriage to excel, in the name of Jesus.

14. O Lord, restore lost glories of my marriage, in the name of Jesus.

15. Let my marriage begin to receive dumbfounding promotions, in the name of Jesus.

16. Let the God of suddenly arise and deliver my marriage from enemies, in the name of Jesus.

17. Every evil speech made against my marriage, be reversed, in the name of Jesus.

18. Any Haman standing against my marriage, die, in the name of Jesus.

19. Any evil done to separate me from my marriage, be frustrated, in the name of Jesus.

20. Any war going on spiritually against my marriage, stop, in the name of Jesus.

21. I command my marriage to receive fresh fire, in the name of Jesus.

22. Let the plans of the devil to dissolve my marriage be terminated, in the name of Jesus.

1. Any evil sentence programmed against my marriage, be reversed, in the name of Jesus.

2. Any satanic counter attack against my marriage, be frustrated, in the name of Jesus.

3. Let every conflict and hostility directed against my marriage die, in the name of Jesus.

4. O Lord, arise and resuscitate my dead marriage, in the name of Jesus.

5. O Lord, bless my marriage and cause me to laugh at last, in the name of Jesus.

6. Father Lord, deliver my marriage from inordinate affections, in the name of Jesus.

7. Any evil hand stretched against my marriage, dry up, in the name of Jesus.

8. I bring the strongman against my marriage to open disgrace, in the name of Jesus.

9. Any death that is already killing in my marriage, die again, in the name of Jesus.

10. Let the blood of Jesus speak my marriage out of shame, in the name of Jesus.

11. Any satanic representation spreading evil against my marriage, die, in the name of Jesus.

12. O Lord, arise and make the enemies of my marriage powerless, in the name of Jesus.

13. Let the spirit of unity reign supreme in my marriage forever, in the name of Jesus.

14. Holy Spirit, arise and incubate my marriage, in the name of Jesus.

15. O Lord, bless my marriage with positive surprises, in the name of Jesus.

16. I command my marriage to begin to harvest miracles, in the name of Jesus.

17. Any evil bridge constructed against my marriage, break, in the name of Jesus.

18. O Lord, send Your power into the foundation of my marriage, in the name of Jesus.

19. Any personal bondage designed especially for my marriage, break, in the name of Jesus.

20. Let the stone of fire break the head of my marriage Goliath, in the name of Jesus.

21. O Lord, give my marriage abundant supply, in the name of Jesus.

22. Let the rod of the wicked over my marriage be broken, in the name of Jesus.

1. Every enemy against the divine vision for my marriage, be destroyed in shame, in the name of Jesus.

2. Let every mermaid spirit working against my marriage be frustrated, in the name of Jesus.

3. Let the Holy anger from above enter into my marriage by fire, in the name of Jesus.

4. Any power promoting problem in my marriage, die by force, in the name of Jesus.

5. Any evil personality that is prospering in my marital problems, be destroyed, in the name of Jesus.

6. Let all the enemies of my marriage be humiliated, in the name of Jesus.

7. Let the judgment of God fall upon the wickedness of the wicked in my marriage, in the name of Jesus.

8. Let the sunrise against every enemy of my marriage, in the name of Jesus.

9. Any evil personality that drinks water and breaths and yet attacks my marriage shall be troubled by water and air, in the name of Jesus.

10. O Lord, arise and deliver my marriage from refuse dumps of the enemy, in the name of Jesus.

11. Let the wind of joy and peace prevail over the enemies of my marriage, in the name of Jesus.

12. I command my marriage to come out from the valley of destruction, in the name of Jesus.

13. Let the forces of the enemy that is surrendering my marriage scatter, in the name of Jesus.

14. I release divine hailstones upon the heads of enemies of my marriage, in the name of Jesus.

15. I command my marriage to move from bondage to liberty, in the name of Jesus.

16. Let the fear of the Lord dominate my marriage forever, in the name of Jesus.

17. Any attack against my marriage from my place of birth, backfire, in the name of Jesus.

18. Lord Jesus, advertize Your glory in my marriage, in the name of Jesus.

19. My life partner will not cooperate with the enemies of my marriage, in the name of Jesus.

20. Every evil command giving to my marriage shall not stand, in the name of Jesus.

21. You my marriage, refuse to assist your enemies, in the name of Jesus.

1. Any strange fire in my marriage, be destroyed by the fire of God, in the name of Jesus.

2. Every seed of poverty wasting my marriage, be wasted by the wrath of God, in the name of Jesus.

3. O Lord, give me a financial breakthrough that will say goodbye to poverty forever, in the name of Jesus.

4. Any demon that breaks marriages, you cannot break my marriage, in the name of Jesus.

5. Any evil pregnancy against my marriage, be aborted by fire, in the name of Jesus.

6. O Lord, make my marriage fruitful at all cost in every good way, in the name of Jesus.

7. Every child born in my marriage, be renewed by fire, in the name of Jesus.

8. Let the youth of my marriage be renewed by fire, in the name of Jesus.

9. Any power that have vowed to kill my partner or me, die immediately, in the name of Jesus.

10. Any arrow of death fired against anyone in my home, backfire, in the name of Jesus.

11. O Lord, provide money for my family to own our own house, in the name of Jesus.

12. I command my marriage to prevail and be example of peace to every other marriage, in the name of Jesus.

13. Let my prayers become atomic bomb to all her enemies, in the name of Jesus.

14. Any power using sex to attack my marriage, be disgraced, in the name of Jesus.

15. I command the spirit of dog militating against my marriage to die, in the name of Jesus.

16. I with draw my marriage from the palace of demonic immorality, in the name of Jesus.

17. Father Lord, deliver my marriage from interventions of spirits against marriages, in the name of Jesus.

18. Let my prayer life become acidic to my family problems, in the name of Jesus.

19. Any warfare going on against my marriage, be terminated to our favor, in the name of Jesus.

20. I command every demonic action taken against my marriage to fail, in the name of Jesus.

21. Let every satanic network against my marriage begin to fail, in the name of Jesus.

22. Blood of Jesus, speak my marriage out of captivity, in the name of Jesus.

23. Let the head of Haman of my marriage be cut off, in the name of Jesus.

24. O Lord, help my marriage to locate all her helpers, in the name of Jesus.

1. Any financial demonic lack in my marriage, disappear forever, in the name of Jesus.

2. Any arrow of demotion fired against my marriage, I fire you back, in the name of Jesus.

3. Any power that has vowed to assassinate my marriage, be disgraced by fire, in the name of Jesus.

4. Every evil conspiracy against my marriage, be put to shame, in the name of Jesus.

5. Every yoke of hardship placed upon my marriage, break to pieces, in the name of Jesus.

6. Every impending loss planned by unfriendly friends against my family, I block your way, in the name of Jesus.

7. Any wreck planned by my unfriendly friends against my marriage , be disappointed, in the name of Jesus.

8. Let every seed of lust targeted to destroy my marriage die, in the name of Jesus.

9. I break and loose my marriage from the banner of sickness and diseases, in the name of Jesus.

10. O Lord, if my marriage is not where it is supposed to be, take it to the right place, in the name of Jesus.

11. Every arrow of premature death fired against my marriage, backfire, in the name of Jesus.

12. Any satanic fire that has captured any area of my marriage, scatter and die, in the name of Jesus.

13. Every spirit of anger and demonic temper working against my marriage, be destroyed, in the name of Jesus.

14. Every demonic gang up and hostility against my marriage, scatter, in the name of Jesus.

15. Any evil covenant or initiation affecting my marriage, expire, in the name of Jesus.

16. Blood of Jesus, enter into my marriage's foundation and cleanse it by force, in the name of Jesus.

17. Every demon of annoyance and oppression against my marriage, I cast you out, in the name of Jesus.

18. Every demonic danger ahead of my marriage, be cleared away, in the name of Jesus.

19. I cast out every spirit of bitterness and misunderstanding against my marriage, in the name of Jesus.

20. O Lord, arise and silence every problem in my marriage by fire, in the name of Jesus.

21. Blood of Jesus, empower my marriage to experience every good change, in the name of Jesus.

22. I command my marriage to discover and recover every good thing it lost, in the name of Jesus.

23. Let divine protection and security begin to fall upon my marriage, in the name of Jesus.

1. Father Lord, empower my marriage to experience love and happiness by fire, in the name of Jesus.

2. Let every bad habit assigned to destroy my marriage die by fire, in the name of Jesus.

3. O Lord, help my marriage to be lifted up by new friends and sincere helpers,

4. Let the wind of divine change enter into my family by fire, in the name of Jesus.

5. Blood of Jesus, empower my marriage to experience victory and elevations, in the name of Jesus.

6. Good success and prosperity, enter into my family by fire, in the name of Jesus.

7. Let my marriage enter into seasons of comfort and peace, in the name of Jesus.

8. Let the spirit of fear upon my marriage depart forever, in the name of Jesus.

9. Any evil spirit pursing my marriage out of her comfort zone, I cast you out, in the name of Jesus.

10. Let every yoke of marine witchcraft against my marriage break, in the name of Jesus.

11. Any satanic counter attack from the waters against my marriage, fail, in the name of Jesus.

12. Every ancestral evil flow into my marriage, expire, in the name of Jesus.

13. Every curse of marital failure upon my marriage, expire, in the name of Jesus.

14. O Lord, arise and perfect Your will upon my marriage, in the name of Jesus.

15. Any evil blood crying against my marriage, be silenced by the blood of Jesus, in the name of Jesus.

16. Let evil altars of my place of birth against my marriage be burnt to ashes, in the name of Jesus.

17. I remove my marriage from the grip of collective captivity, in the name of Jesus.

18. Father Lord, deliver my marriage from destructive covenants and curses, in the name of Jesus.

19. Let every germ, spiritually or physically in my marriage die, in the name of Jesus.

20. Let the spirit of snail in my marriage be cast out forever, in the name of Jesus.

21. Any household witchcraft attacking my marriage, be disgraced, in the name of Jesus.

22. O Lord, arise and command my marriage to excel by fire, in the name of Jesus.

23. Any yoke upon my marriage, break, in the name of Jesus.

24. Blood of Jesus, set my marriage free from all evil forces, in the name of Jesus.

1. Any evil stone, spiritually or physically, blocking my marriage from success, be removed, in the name of Jesus.

2. Any evil power assigned to kill the destiny of my marriage, die immediately, in the name of Jesus.

3. Every defeat my marriage has ever suffered, be converted to victory, in the name of Jesus.

4. I release my marriage from the house of the strongman, in the name of Jesus.

5. Every good door closed against my marriage, be opened by force, in the name of Jesus.

6. Every spirit against peace and harmony in my marriage, be wasted, in the name of Jesus.

7. Any satanic reinforcement against my marriage, scatter, in the name of Jesus.

8. I command the strongman sitting upon my marriage to leave by fire, in the name of Jesus.

9. Let my marriage begin to experience open heaven by fire, in the name of Jesus.

10. O Lord, arise and take my marriage to the mountaintop of joy and peace, in the name of Jesus.

11. I command the power of God to prosper to enter into my marriage, in the name of Jesus.

12. O Lord, put Your divine honey into my marriage by fire, in the name of Jesus.

13. Any evil hand shaking the pillars of my marriage, dry up, in the name of Jesus.

14. O Lord, help my marriage win every competition, in the name of Jesus.

15. Power to retain the presence of God forever, fall upon my marriage, in the name of Jesus.

16. Any power that wants to move my marriage out of her place, die, in the name of Jesus.

17. O Lord, empower my marriage to bear fruit in season and out of season, in the name of Jesus.

18. I cut off every evil link in my marriage, in the name of Jesus.

19. Let the spirit of religion and falsehood depart from my marriage, in the name of Jesus.

20. I command my marriage to enjoy God's true liberty from above, in the name of Jesus.

21. Let my marriage begin to experience supernatural breakthroughs, in the name of Jesus.

22. I break every yoke of evil flow into my marriage, in the name of Jesus.

23. Father Lord, send Your flesh fire from above into my marriage, in the name of Jesus.

24. Let my marriage begin to enjoy holy disturbances from heaven, in the name of Jesus.

1. I deliver my marriage from the bondage of inordinate affections and soul- ties, in the name of Jesus.

2. Blood of Jesus, flow into my marriage and safeguard my home, in the name of Jesus.

3. Any evil plan to separate my marriage, be frustrated, in the name of Jesus.

4. I cast out from my marriage every spirit of divorce, in the name of Jesus.

5. Let every yoke of marital crisis in my home break to piece, in the name of Jesus.

6. Every evil arrest of my marriage by home destroyers, be terminated, in the name of Jesus.

7. O Lord, put Your abundant life upon my dead marriage, in the name of Jesus.

8. I command my marriage to be delivered from foundational pollution, in the name of Jesus.

9. Let Jesus my redeemer take over my marriage forever and ever, in the name of Jesus.

10. Every serpent and scorpion upon my marriage, I tread upon you by fire, in the name of Jesus.

11. Father Lord, release Your dumb founding breakthroughs into my marriage, in the name of Jesus.

12. Every evil decree tormenting my marriage, be revoked, in the name of Jesus.

13. Let every area of my marriage receive great deliverance, in the name of Jesus.

14. Every hidden problem in my marriage, be exposed and disgraced, in the name of Jesus.

15. Anointing to excel, fall upon my marriage by fire, in the name of Jesus.

16. Every aggressive and unrepentant enemy of my marriage, die, in the name of Jesus.

17. Let the full glory of God return back into my marriage, in the name of Jesus.

18. Any demonic action taken against my marriage, be frustrated, in the name of Jesus.

19. Let the head of the strongman in my marriage be cut off forever, in the name of Jesus.

20. Father Lord, command my marriage to experience Your own elevation today,

21. Any evil power, contending with the glory of my marriage, die, in the name of Jesus.

22. Holy Ghost fire, burn to ashes every enemy of my marriage, in the name of Jesus.

1. Every satanic plan to kill and destroy the peace in my marriage, be frustrated, in the name of Jesus.

2. Any demonic eraser designed to erase divine deposited love in my marriage, die, in the name of Jesus.

3. Any fake lion scattering divine plan for my marriage, die, in the name of Jesus.

4. I command every presence of stagnation in my marriage to disappear, in the name of Jesus.

5. Any witchcraft animal programmed into my marriage, die, in the name of Jesus.

6. Let traps enemies have set to catch my marriage catch its agents, in the name of Jesus.

7. Let confusion swallow every enemy of my marriage, in the name of Jesus.

8. Every demonic serpent attacking my marriage, stretch forth and die, in the name of Jesus.

9. Every evil egg laid against my marriage, break to pieces, in the name of Jesus.

10. Every enemy of God's reign upon my marriage, be disgrace by force, in the name of Jesus.

11. Let satanic armed robbers in my marriage begin to die one by one, in the name of Jesus.

12. I command the mouths of demonic lions in my marriage to be padlocked, in the name of Jesus.

13. Let the senses of all the enemies of my marriage receive confusion, in the name of Jesus.

14. Let all the soldiers of the devil raised against my marriage die, in the name of Jesus.

15. Every good blessing that is dormant in my marriage, receive life, in the name of Jesus.

16. Any strange power fighting against my marriage, be disgraced by force, in the name of Jesus.

17. O Lord, empower my marriage to survive every demonic attack, in the name of Jesus.

18. Let divine favor and God's love possess my marriage forever, in the name of Jesus.

19. Let every Goliath against my marriage die in shame and disgrace, in the name of Jesus.

20. Every witchcraft weapon prepared against my marriage, catch fire, in the name of Jesus.

21. Every satanic representative in my marriage, die immediately, in the name of Jesus.

22. Every wicked spirit militating against my marriage, be cast out, in the name of Jesus.

1. Whether my enemies like it or not, my marriage must survive every trial, in the name of Jesus.

2. Every seed of non-achievement germinating in the corridors of my marriage, die, in the name of Jesus.

3. Any evil pot cooking my marriage, break to pieces, in the name of Jesus.

4. Any evil chain holding my marriage down with all manner of problems, break, in the name of Jesus.

5. Let every satanic worm in the root of my marriage die, in the name of Jesus.

6. Any sexual relationship in the spirit or physical designed to destroy my marriage, be destroyed, in the name of Jesus.

7. Blood of Jesus, open a new chapter of progress in my marriage, in the name of Jesus.

8. I command my marriage to jump out from the pit of disgrace, in the name of Jesus.

9. Every witchcraft tree standing against my marriage, be cut down, in the name of Jesus.

10. Every evil foundation my marriage is standing upon, I pull you down, in the name of Jesus.

11. By the power in the name of Jesus, I build a new foundation for my marriage, in the name of Jesus.

12. Any power covering the glory of my marriage, be disgraced, in the name of Jesus.

13. Let the finished wine of my marriage be replaced by the wine of Jesus, in the name of Jesus.

14. O Lord, return my marriage to the days of her honeymoon, in the name of Jesus.

15. O Lord, send Your helpers into my marriage today, in the name of Jesus.

16. Every enemy of my marriage, be disgraced by fire, in the name of Jesus.

17. Every seed of confusion and failure fired against my marriage, backfire, in the name of Jesus.

18. Let the original vision of God for my marriage begin to manifest, in the name of Jesus.

19. Any water spirit attacking my marriage, be disgraced by death, in the name of Jesus.

20. Every opposition in my marriage, die, in the name of Jesus.

21. Father Lord, bring wonderful changes into my marriage, in the name of Jesus.

22. Every mountain of impossibility standing against my marriage, disappear, in the name of Jesus.

23. Any spiritual or physical sabotage against my marriage, be disgraced, in the name of Jesus.

Thank You So Much!

Beloved, I hope you enjoyed this Book as much as I believe God has touched your heart today. I cannot thank you enough for your continued support for this prayer ministry.

I appreciate you so much for taking out of time to read this wonderful prayer book, and if you have an extra second, I would love to hear what you think about this book.

Please, do share your testimonies with me by sending an email to me at pastor@prayermadueke.com, also in Facebook at www.facebook.com/prayer.madueke. I personally invite you to my website at www.prayermadueke.com to view many other books I have written on various issues of life, especially on marriage, family, sexual problems and money.

I will be delighted to partner with you in organized Crusades, Ceremonies, Marriages and Marriage seminars, Special Events, Church Ministration and Fellowship for the advancement of God's Kingdom here on earth.

Thank you again, and I wish you nothing less than success in life.

God bless you.

Prayer M. Madueke

OTHER BOOKS BY PRAYER M. MADUEKE

- *21/40 Nights Of Decrees And Your Enemies Will Surrender*
- *Confront And Conquer*
- *35 Special Dangerous Decrees*
- *Tears in Prison*
- *The Reality of Spirit Marriage*
- *Queen of Heaven*
- *Leviathan the Beast*
- *100 Days Prayer To Wake Up Your Lazarus*
- *Dangerous Decrees To Destroy Your Destroyers*
- *The spirit of Christmas*
- *More Kingdoms To Conquer*
- *Your Dream Directory*
- *The Sword Of New Testament Deliverance*
- *Alphabetic Battle For Unmerited Favors*
- *Alphabetic Character Deliverance*
- *Holiness*
- *The Witchcraft Of The Woman That Sits Upon Many Waters*
- *The Operations Of The Woman That Sits Upon Many Waters*
- *Powers To Pray Once And Receive Answers*
- *Prayer Riots To Overthrow Divorce*
- *Prayers To Get Married Happily*
- *Prayers To Keep Your Marriage Out of Troubles*
- *Prayers For Conception And Power To Retain*
- *Prayer Retreat – Prayers to Possess Your Year*
- *Prayers for Nation Building (Vol. 1,2 & 3)*
- *Organized student in a disorganized school*
- *Welcome to Campus*
- *Alone with God (10 series)*

CONTACTS

AFRICA

#1 Babatunde close,
Off Olaitan Street, Surulere
Lagos, Nigeria
+234 803 353 0599
pastor@prayermadueke.com,

#28B Ubiaja Crescent
Garki II Abuja,
FCT - Nigeria
+234 807 065 4159

IRELAND

Ps Emmanuel Oko
#84 Thornfield Square
Cloudalkin D22
Ireland
Tel: +353 872 820 909, +353 872 977 422
aghaoko2003@yahoo.com

EUROPE/SCHENGEN

Collins Kwame
#46 Felton Road
Barking
Essex IG11 7XZ GB
Tel: +44 208 507 8083, +44 787 703 2386, +44 780 703 6916
aghaoko2003@yahoo.com